A SANTAL THEOLOGY OF LIBERATION

"Towards the rising of the sun was the birth of man"

—*Santal creation myth*

A Santal Theology of Liberation

V. MANUEL RAJ

UPPAL PUBLISHING HOUSE
NEW DELHI—110002

UPPAL PUBLISHING HOUSE
3, Ansari Road, Daryaganj, New Delhi-110002

First Edition 1990
IBSN 81-85024-81-3

Copies are available :
The Santal Welfare and Cultural Society Mayapuri,
New Delhi-110064.

Printed in India

Published by B.S. Uppal, Uppal Publishing House
3, Ansari Road, Daryaganj, New Delhi-110002
Printed at Sainion Printary, Delhi - 11 00 32.

Dedicated

to

My beloved Santals

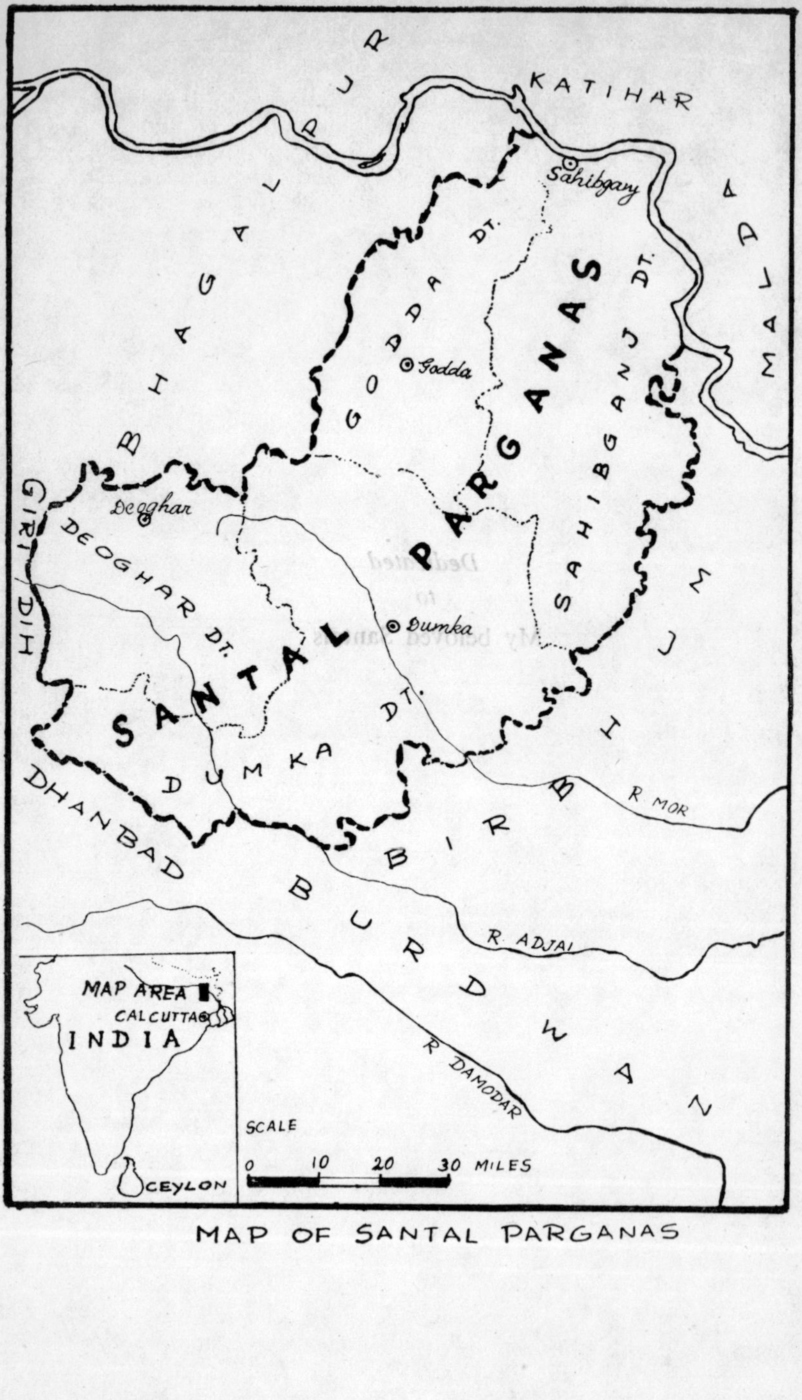

MAP OF SANTAL PARGANAS

A Santal Folk-Song

Santal Pargana ho sona disom
Bir-buru te gada-sodok′ te
Dare nã̤ṛite sajao-akan.
Ato simko rag sãote bir cẽṛẽko cero bero
Manwako rag sãote-2
Chandoe goṅa.

Translation :

Santal Pargana the golden land
With woods and hills
Meandering rivers and springs
Trees and creepers adorned.

With village roosters' whooping
Mingles forest birds' chirping
With human cry-2
Rises the 'Chando' in response.

Foreword

The Santals are the single largest tribal group in India. By their sheet number...eight million people, that is 1% of the Indian population—they claim our attention—attention to what is happening to them. This tribal people, with unique cultural characteristics, have all along been harassed, oppressed and exploited by the 'diku' landlords, the money-lenders and by the political powers. They have been deprived of their lands, their forests—the sources of their survival.

But the Santals are not a people acquiescent and resigned to their lot. They havd been a struggling people. Like the *Minjung*, the oppressed people of Korea, and like the blacks of South Africa, the Santals are active agents of their own liberation. A deep awareness and even assertion of their cultural identity is indispensable in the project of their liberation. Loss of cultural identity is loss of their freedom, just like the loss of their lands and forests is the loss of the physical as well as spiritual means of their survival. In the case of the Santals, their culture and freedom—the spiritual dimension, so to say,—is inextricably intertwined with their lands and forests—the material and the earthly sources of life.

At the global level, the experience of the last few years show a remarkable shift taking place from the economic and the political towards the cultural which is beginning to occupy the central stage in the struggles for liberation. The Santals have to draw from their cultural resources the strength to withstand and overcome the evil forces that continue to keep them in bondage. The Santals have also a lot to draw from their own history. They resisted and fought fiercely their oppressors in many rebellions, specially in the well-known 'hul' (rebellion) in 1855-1857.

The movement of liberation and struggle among the Santals has not been in vain. It has borne fruits, the most significant of which is the creation of a homeland for themselves—the Santal Parganas. Once again, despite ominous signs of Santal identity being wiped out and their liberation movement brutally repressed, in recent times, fresh signs of hope are re-appearing. The determination of the Santals not to surrender themselves to their exploiters is growing stronger. Peoples' victory over the dictatorial regime and the volcanic outburst of the Romanian people in recent days against the iron fisted misrule of Ceausescu and his wife Elena, leading to their overthrowing and execution is people's power at work. It should serve as a warning to all those who-think that they can continue to exploit with impunity the tribals of the country.

A theology of liberation among the Santals has to grown out of their experience and sufferings, their struggles and revolts, hopes and dreams. It has to sustain them in their fight for self-determination and liberation. This book offers inspiration for the development of a Santal theology of liberation, rooted in their culture, tradition and history. From the point of view of methodology, it wants to read the Bible starting from the experience of Santals, and not the other way round. It critically surveys also the involvement of the Church among the Santals and calls for inculturation in all areas of the life of the Church. Only such an inculturated Church can be truly an involved participant in their project of liberation.

Anthropologists are wont to distinguish beetween 'etic' and 'emic' approach to a culture, according to whether it is studied from without as a phenomenon or looked at from within, making oneself a part of the culture of the people studied. What the author of this book, Manuel Raj, has attempted, in my view, goes even further than an emic approach. But for his biological origin he is a Santal among whom he was reborn anew. For the past sixteen years he has made himself one with the Santals and their cause. His attempt to develop a Santal theology of liberation is the result of his own experience as one of them.

The contribution this book makes is very significant, and it cannot be passed over by anyone who is interested and involved in the life and destiny of this unique Indian tribals—the Santals.

Tiruchirapalli
15.8.1990

Felix Wilfred
Member of the International
Theological Commission.

Preface

"A Santal Theology of Liberation" by V. Manuel Raj, S.J.
has been a challenging endeavour,
not only for the missionaries working among the Santals
but also for all the social workers and volunatary organisations
that associate themselves with the development of the Santals.

The book begins with an indepth study of our (the Santal) community, it critically analyses the socio-economic, cultural, political as well as religious aspects of our society.

We have been at the receving end for years.
Socially and culturally we have been suppressed
and not allowed to develop and prosper.
Economically and politically we have been plundered
year after year. The abundant wealth and resources of 'Sona Santal Pargana' has attracted 'dikus' (non-Santals) from every where in enormous number.

They (dikus) have exploited us,
plundered us, used us
and ultimately have enslaved us
and made us homeless
and alien in our own homeland. Can we think of a worse
tragedy than this ?

The factors responsible for pushing the Santal society into a wilderness of poverty have been aptly identified in this book.

No doubt before independence it started with the advent of unscrupulous money-lenders or the 'diku' mahajons into the Santal Regions. These, together with the cruel 'diku' tax-collector and the barbic police, reigned over the peace-loving Santals. But "amidst all these intollerable oppression there was also a yearning deep down in the heart of every Santal for independence and for recognition as masters of the soil".

This inherent yearning coupled with barbaric rule meted out to the Santals culminated in the historic Santal Rebellion of 1855-1857 better known as the 'HUL'.

This historic event has been very vividly brought out in this book.

The sacrifice of the thousands
of Santal lives in the 'HUL'
did have a few far reaching results.

A distinct administrative territory namely 'Santal Parganas' with Head quarted at Dumka was carved out of the then Bhagalpur and Birbhum districts.

The transfer of land from a Santal owner to a diku was declared illegal. At last we '*had*' a land of our own-the 'Sona Santal Pargana'.

But what is the present scenario ?

Well, the district of Santal Pargana does no longer exist. It has been broken up into pieces on the pretext of better administration. The lush green forests with billions of trees have disappeared. The springs have long been dried up.

Our golden land has been savagely ravaged and raped bitterly. And who is to blame for this sad state of affairs ?

It is no doubt the 'dikus'
the 'diku' money-lenders,
the 'diku' administration,
the shallow government policy
and the 'diku' law
that has been imposed upon us till this day.

The question now is :

How do we liberate ourselves from our oppressors ?
Is spiritual liberation or salvation complete in itself without caring for the socio-econmic and political liberation ?

I firmly believe that the spiritual liberation and the
liberation from the socio-economic and cultural
oppression are
but two sides of the same coin.

A spiritual liberation alone in itself is meaningless. It acquires its true meaning only when it enables a community to break free from the shackles of age old oppression and allows it to prosper and preserve its socio-cultural identity.

In this context, I feel V. Manuel Raj
has rightly pointed out
that there is a strong need
for a different theology
for the salvation of the Santals—
not a 'diku' (foreign) theology
but only an indigenous,
'HOṚ THEOLOGY'.

Dr. D. Marndi
Secretary,
Santhal welfare and
cultural society,
New-Delhi.

Ackonwledgements

It has been my intense desire to intitate a theology that is specific to the Santals. This small book in your hands is the result of that deep yearning and of the present day need of the Santal Church.

My thanks to the sustained goodwill and encouragement of many of my friends and Jesuit companions.

My sincere gratitude goes to my brother Fr. V. Richard, Director, Social-Development-Centre, Dumka and to Fr. Josephraj, S.J., Liberatian, Vidyajoyti, Delhi who helped me in many ways in bringing this book out into being.

I am indebted to the numerous scholars who have made their invaluable works available for me and to sevral others who were unselfish in their help.

Finally, I want to extend a special word of thanks to my people, the Santals, who affectionately made known to me the intricacies of their life and whose love I cherish.

Dumka
1.5.1990

V. Manuel Raj

Ackonwledgements

It has been my intense desire to initiate a theology that is [illegible] to the Santals. The small book in your hands is the result of that deep yearning and of the present day need of the Santal Church.

My thanks to the sustained goodwill and encouragement of many of my friends and fellow companions.

My sincere gratitude goes to my brother Fr. V. Rajagopal, Director, Social Development Centre, Dumka and to Fr. [illegible] Librarian, Vidyajyoti, Delhi who helped me in many ways in bringing this book out into being.

I am indebted to the numerous scholars who have made valuable works available to me and to several others who were [illegible] with their help.

Finally, I want to extend a special word of thanks to my people, the Santals who affectionately made known to me the intricacies of their life and [illegible].

Dumka V. Manuel Raj
1-5-1990

Contents

Introduction

"............let justice roll down like waters, and righteousness like an ever-flowing stream." (Am. 5 : 24)

This has never been the ground-rule of action of any ruling class in Santal-Parganas. While I sit to spill some ink on the paper, I'm reminded of a saying of Malcolm : "Don't let anybody who is oppressing us ever lay the ground-rules. Let them know now that this is a new game, and we've got some new rules...."[1]. Gone are the days when the Santals lived a fatalistic life. This is not an era where the oppressed Santals look-up to their oppressors to give them some system of logic or reason. What is logical to the 'dikus' is no logic to them. And what is reason to their oppressors is no reason for the oppressed. As the Santals today, more than ever, are realizing that what sounds reasonable and logical to their exploiters is neither reasonable nor logical to them, the time is ripe now to devise a system, a set of rules to re-place the old. This alone can bear some fruit in their struggle for freedom. And I term this struggle as "Santal-Revolution".

The 'Santalness' in the land of Santals has become a power of Liberation today. The Santal theology of liberation in today's context therefore, must be evoking the spirit of Santalness. Theology in this light becomes an on-going attempt of this particular community to define in every generation its reason for being in the world. There can never be a universal theology.

It is essentially boundup with a particular community. The theology of the oppressors cannot be an authentic theology, for its interest is one of maintaining the statusquo. This, in the term of James Cone, is an anti-Christ theology. An authentic Christian theology is the theology of the oppressed people. God-talk can never be a christian-talk until and unless it is amalgamated with the liberation of the oppressed. My deep conviction as that of Cone is that no Santal should be claiming to do theology today unless the focal point and purpose of her/his theology is the liberative praxis of the Santals.

The responsibility for the Santal societal change is an essential part of the Santal theological task today. This little book is a drop in the great ocean of the challenging task every Santal theologian is faced with. This may ebb controversies and may even make the oppressive communities raise their eyebrows. This is precisely why theologizing has become a very dangerous job today. An authentic theologian has to be obedient to the Word of God and faithful in doing it, even to the point of death on the cross. He believes that the death of Jesus is not the end of everything but the beginning of a new life. God, raising Jesus from death has called humanity to a new hope.

V. Manuel Raj

CHAPTER 1

The Santals

In Midnapur district of West-Bengal, about seven hundred and fifty kilo-metres west of Damin-i-koh, lay the land of Saont. It was the occupants of the land who have acquired the name Santals. The Santals, an agrarian cum pastoral nomadic community were not called by that name till they occupied the land of Saont. According to tradition, their ancestors come to this land as immigrants form the "Champa Disom" (probably the country which lies to the north-west of the Chotanagpur plateau). Interestingly it were the foreigners who gave them the name "Santal" pertaining to the land of which they were residents for some time. The Hindi form "Santal" or the Bengali form "Saotar" does seem to describe them as a people belonging to Saont or Saot.

The creation of Santal-Parganas was a direct sequal to the Santal Rebellion of 1855-57, when special system of administration to safeguard the interest of the Santals, the Non-Regulation Act XXXVII of 1857, was passed. According to this Act an area of 5,470 Sq. miles was carved out of Bhagalpur and Birbhum districts to constitute Santal-Parganas. As per the Santal-Parganas Land Tenancy Act of 1855, the ownership of the land of the Santals is not transferable to any non-Santals.

As the name implies, Santal-Parganas is the home-land for the Santal tribe in India. The scheduled tribe population is approximately 37% of the total population and the Santals represent about 86% of the total scheduled tribe population in Santal-Parganas.

VITAL STATISTICS

Total Area	:	14,129 Sp. Kms.
Cultivable land	:	18,85,618 acres
Barren land	:	18,15,182 ,,
Forest	:	3,60,422 ,,
Rainfall	:	1,377.2 m.m.
Total Population	:	37,15,376
(a) Sch. Caste	:	306, 294
(b) Sch. Tribes	:	1,267,807
Precentage of		
(a) Sch. Caste	:	7.2
(b) Sch. Tribes	:	36.8
Density of population per Sq. km.	:	226

THE SANTALS : A BIRD'S EYE-VIEW

There are more than 8 million Santals in the Indian sub-continent.

They represent 8 times the Naga population
10 ,, ,, Khasis &
14 ,, ,, Gharos.

They are more numerous than the Mundas
Oraons
Hos & Kharias & all the three categories put together.

They are 1% of India's total population and 13% of tribal population (60 million).

The bulk of Santals live in Blhar	:	3 million
Bengal	:	2 ,,
Orissa	:	1 ,,
(North-Western) Assam	:	4 Lakhs
(Dinajpur diocese) Bangladesh	:	2, 500

(in regions bordering Purena & Nepal : a few thousands)

(SANTAL POPULATION IN SANTAL-PARGANAS)

		Growth %
1901	18,04,526	
1911	19,77,486	+ 4.04
1921	17,93,742	− 4.46
1931	20,50,258	+ 14.30
1941	22,34,407	+ 8.99
1951	23,22,292	+ 3.92
1961	26,75,205	+ 15.21
1971	37,42,805	+ 34.4

(Dumka District)

1. The population growth since 1901-1961 (60 years) is 8 lakhs whereas during 1961-1981 (20 years) it is 15 lakhs.
2. During the perod 1961 1981 (20 years) 2 lakhs migrated to Bengal, Assam and Punjab due to poverty.
3. Of the 15 lakhs majority are from North Bihar Districts.

Source : District Gazette 1965 and District Handbook 1986.

Every society, either micro or macro, consists of two systems: Organzation-system and Meaning-systen. The Organization-system comprises of economic, political, and social aspects of society. The meaning system comprises of religious, cultural and ideological factors of society. Money is said to be or considered to be only a means. But today, in all societies with an exception of a few, money has become the moving factor that influences all the other aspects of society. It has become "the God" of the people. And it has created great disparities between the rich and the poor; the haves and the have-nots.

CHAPTER 2

A Critical Analysis of the Economic, Socio-Religious and Political Life of the Santals

The Economic Life of the Santals :

The Santal culture is basically a village culture revolving round agriculture. Agriculture is the back-bone of the village economy, and predominant occupation of the bulk of the aboriginal Santal population. It is, in fact, the very foundation of the village culture.

Santal life is greatly conditioned and influenced by forest on which they depend for their supply of food, fodder, animals, fuelwood, building and materials for tools and medicine. Forest is also an important source of their income from which they obtain edible oil-seeds, and timber and fuelwood for trading in the market. The importance of forest for the Santals is obvious from the fact that there is a close relationship between the distribution of Santal population and the distribution of forest area in the State of Bihar. The districts with large area under forest also have a large tribal population. For example, the

Santal Parganas—Chotanagpur region which accounts for nearly 70% of the forest area in the state is also the region where about 90% of the tribal population is concentrated. 3,60,422 acres out of the total area 14,129 Sq. km (5470 Sq. miles) of Santal Parganas is forest.

It is a great irony, however, that while the Santal population derives its livelihood from the forest, the state's forest area is greatly denuded. There is large scale deforestation on account of reckless felling of trees by the contractors under the prevalent leasing system.

The forests, the habitat of the Santals, become a prey for industry, commerce and colonial ambitions. The British legalized forest exploitation by passing a number of Forest Acts in which vested interests gained while the voiceless Santals found themselves bereft of their traditional inhabitat.

Following Independence, forests play an important role in industrial growth. Deforestation get maximized as the forest provides raw material for forest-based industries. As industries and technologies develop, demands out strip supply. The Government's forest policies have been favourable to the non-tribals and the government officials. It is true that the government has launched wide-spread aforestation programmes. However, this does not reflect the concern for the enviornmental and people-based needs. The government does not take care of the Minor Forest Produce on which the poor Santals depend. Deforestation has also affected the geo-ecological balance in tribal areas. It has led to the decline of soil fertility, and change of climate to a very great extent.

Subsequently, the Santals can no more follow their traditional pursuit of hunting and fruit gathering. This has stripped off the subsidiary income of the Santals. It is, therefore, their great interest in wet-rice cultivation and permanent agriculture that has formed focal economic interest in the Santal culture. 18,85,618 acres of land in Santal Parganas is cultivable. And almost 98% of the Santal population is dependent on agriculture as cultivators or as agricultural labourers.

The average annual rainfall in Santal Parganas is 54.2 inches, 83 per cent of which occurs between June and September. But they come down in flood and become rapid torrents, impassable owing to the velocity of the current. Besides the Ganges there are other important rivers such as Gumani, Bansloi, Brahmani, Adjoy, Mar and Mayurakshi. But the presence of these rivers have made only a little perceptible change to the economy of the people, because except the Ganges, other rivers are of seasonal in nature.

Poor irrigational facilities have resulted in lower percentage of area under cultivation and lower cropping intensity. While the total irrigated areas in the districts of Singhbhum and Santal Parganas stood at 5.20 per cent and 12.04 per cent respectively in 1959-60, it has declined to 4.20 and 7.70 at the end of 1979-80. Cultivators who had constituted 78.1 per cent of the total population in 1961 declined to 63.06 per cent in 1981, whereas agricultural labourers increased from 9.54 per cent to 23.20 during the same period.

Thus there is a clear trend that a substantial Santal population is moving out of the cultivating class. This trend may be attributed to the fact that the land is passing hands from the Santals to non-Santals and also due to the problem of alienation facing the Santal population.

As any other agrarian society, the Santals have great attachment to their land. Land is their life-blood. It is for the land their ancestors shed their blood in the 'hul'. It has a great sentimental value attached. A Santal considers it a dignity to possess a piece of land. Therefore, anyone who lays hand on their land is taken to be laying hand on their very life.

In the rural agrarian society of India, the top 10 per cent own 56 per cent of land while the bottom 50 per cent own only 12 per cent. But the queer thing about the Santal agrarian society is that this disparity is not within their own society but is in relationsip with the 'diku' money-lenders. Mortgaging of land for a little money is prevalent in Santal society even today.

Since the tribals are not able to appreciate the value of their land-holdings as they are unproductive, in times of famine and other needs, large plots of their cultivable land get mortgaged beyond redemption to meney-lenders, Mahajons and to non-tribals. Often the land once mortgaged is lost forever to the tricky benefaction of the outsiders. Above all, the bonded-labour system squeezes the blood out of the debtor. A Santal may cultivate his land, but the product of his labour would go to the creditor. Cases of Santal families cultivating their land for their 'diku' creditor for years together for a little money they owe him is not rare in Santal Parganas. The Hindu money-lenders' exploitation has changed Santals' mode of life and economy to a considerable extent.

Ever since the Santals settled in the land of Saont, they have been constantly facing the terrible tragedy of land alienation. Their land has been torn into bits and pieces by the Hindu money-lenders and by the Indian Government. As the consequence of the Santal 'hul' (1855-57), an Act was passed by the British Government to ensure the non-transferability of the Santal land. This Act was later endorsed by the Indian Govern ment. Provisions are also made in the Constitution of India to safeguard the tribals against such exploitation and alienation. Article 46 in the Chapter on Directive Principles of State Policy states :

> "The state shall promote with special care the educational and economic interests of the weaker sections of the people, and, in particular, of scheduled castes and the scheduled tribes, and shall protect them from social injustice and all forms of exploitation."

The second fundanental principle enumerated in the Tribal 'Panche sheel' as laid down by Nehru the first Prime-Minister of India way back in 1958 is emphatic in this regard. It says :

"Tribal rights in land and forest should be respected". Despite all these that are supposed to safeguard the land of the Santals, more and more of the tribal land is being bought for a pittance by greedy businessmen and government servants coming in to serve themselves in Santal Parganas. Such factors obviously remain as a feeling of molten lava in the minds and hreats of the Santals today.

LAND ALIENATION BY MAHAJONS IN SANTAL PARGANAS

(District established in 1855)

a.	1855 ... 1887 ...	30,937	Acres	(by sale)
b.	1887 ... 1905 ...	32,146	,,	
		63,083	,,	
c.	Land in others' possession (found in 1905)	71,401	,,	
	(Macphersom Settlement)	1,34,484	,,	
d.	1905 ——— 1932	35,927	,,	
	(found during Gangres Settlement)	1,70,411	,,	
e.	1932 ——— 1979	54,731	,,	(approx)
		2,25,142	,,	

Since 1855 till date land alienated	:	2,25,142 acres
Land under actual cultivation	;	13,12,087 acres
Percentage of alienation	:	approximately 25%

Sources : Macphersom Settlement Report, Gangres Settlement Report and Present survey (sample).

The tragedy is that the fence itself is eating-up the plants it is protecting. A government that is supposed to protect the land of the Santals is weaning them away from their mother's breast—from their land that is their life-chord.

A very important provision contained in Article 275 (1) of the Constitution assures a state of special grants from its own to revenues meet the cost of schemes of development for promoting the welfare of the scheduled tribes as well as for better administration of the Scheduled Areas in preference to the rest of the areas of that state.

According to Article 339(2), "the executive power of the Union shall extend to the giving of directions to a state as to the drawing up and executive of scheme essential for the welfare of the scheduled tribes of the state".

Similarly, paragraph 5(1) of the Fifth Schedule provides the Governor with exceptional powers to safe-guard the tribals from any Act of Parliament or of the Legislature of the state detrimental to the Tribal interests.

And so, on the one hand, the Goverment has drawn-up schemes and programmes meant for rural backward communities and tribals; on the other hand the majority of the people for whom these facilities are intended do not even know about their existence. Those few who do know are ill-informed about the details. Moreover, villagers are sceptical about availing themselves of Government credit facilities, subsidies, etc. A lot of it is only on paper. For instance, drinking water-wells are said to be available in 9,440 villages. Over 1200 villages of Santal Parganas division including 900 Paharia (another tribe) villages face acute drinking water crisis throughout the year. The Government had released Rs. 2 crore in 1985 for providing safe drinking water in rural and urban areas of the division. But due to the apathy of some senior officers and rampant corrupation at lower levels, the construction work done was of substandard quality and Rs. 75 lakh out of the alotted amount for development was surrendered unutilized.

Even the Government schemes of Dams and mining meant especially for the tribals have far reaching consequences : they keep displacing a large number of tribal settlements. In the process, so much of the cultivable land of the tribals get destroyed or inundated. Nowhere adequate compensation is being made. The process of industrial development taken in the course of over 40 years of planning has hardly touched the fringe of the tribal population. Rather, it has often been alleged, the benefits of the development programmes have mainly been shared by the affluent non-tribal population of the area and misery of the tribal population has actually increased. The Government of India document "Approach to Tribal Development in Sixth Plan", laments :

> In the name of tribal development we have spent a lot of money during the last several plans but when accounting was made at the end of the last period of the safeguards to the tribals in the Constitution, it was found that actual benefits trickled down to the tribals have not been consisent with the promise we have made. Expenditure has not resulted in the benefits that should have accrued to this population. Unfortunately, the developmental programmes for tribal areas did not yield the desired results.

In reality, with the establishment of these projects there is a vicious cycle of backwardness in the tribal region of Bihar. The industries in Santal Parganas are the stone quarries, coalieries and china-clay mines. Over 200,000 of tribals, men, women and children are engaged over-time and are under-paid. Sexual exploitation of women is despicable in these areas besides the health hazards. In their own home-land, the Santals have become a much exploited and cheap labour-force.

The irony of Tribal development is that the tribals are evacuated from their own villages and landholdings to a far off place where they can find no trace of their culture and way of life. It is said that around 25,000 persons are displaced by each major irrigation project. The Rs. 600 crore Rajmahal Project of the Eastern Coalfields Ltd., and the adjacent housing colony comprising of 60,000 houses have destroyed a vast area of fertile land of the Santals. The settlers as usual are not the sons and daughters of the soil, but mostly the north-Biharis and the Bengali-Babus. All these happen in the name of development of the people and of the land and villages which they hold so precious. It is like killing babies to save the world !

To a politician and a technocrat the idea that flooding a plot of land might destroy a culture is incomprehensible. They fail to realize that to a traditional people land is not real estate or a space over which people are moved like objects. Land is memory, a map of one's world, a way of life for which people are willing to die. That is why the tribals in Gujarat lament :

This land is where we belong—it is God's gift to us and has made us as we are. This land is where we are at home; we know its way; and the things that happen here are known and remembered, so that the stories the old people are still alive here...This land is the place where we know where to find all that it provided for us—food for hunting and fishing, and farms, building and tools, materials, medicines. Also that spirit around us know us and are friendly and helpful.... If we had to move, we would be lost to those who remain in other villages. This would be a sadness to us all, like the sadness of death.

There is scarcely a scheme in existence which has avoided the twin problems of cultural disruption and social alienation.

LAND ALIENATION BY GOVERNMENT IN SANTAL-PARGANAS AND CHOTANAGPUR

Big Projects : TATA, BOKARO, SINDRI

Irrigation Projects : North Koel, Swarna Rekha, Oranga, Ajay, Punasi, Sundar Dam, Torai Reservoir, (*Maithon*, *Panchet*, *Tenughat*)

DVC, Masanjore, Koyalkaro, Kanhan, Burhai etc.

Total Schemes : *153 projects in S. P. Chotanagpur*

1. *Since Independence till 1986*

    a. 11,83,000 peasants wiped away. (Projects other than D.V.C. Masanjore)

    b· 1,50,000 peasants wiped away. (D.V.C.)

    c. 1,00,000 peasants wiped away. (Masanjore)

    ———
    14,33,000

2. *During 75-76 to 1981-'82*

    7. 29 lakh hectare agricultural land submerged.

3. *During 75-76 to 81-82*

    5.86 lakh M.T. foodgrain production dropped.

Source : Water Resource Dept. Budget for 1989-90 (South Bihar).

Oppressions of these kinds have driven the Santals to extreme poverty and misery. However, the tribal solidarity extends a helping-hand to those who are driven to that stage. At the same time the tribal jealousy brings low those who are rich by means of witch-craft etc.

The Santals originally had a barter system of economy. They had subsistence economy. Santal society produced all they needed (except salt for which they used to go to the bazaar, "hat"—mainly a meeting place)—even cloths. The Santal myth about the Kisku raja's servant-girl has a trace of it The myth goes like this :

In the olden days, rice grew ready to be eaten, cotton-plants brought forth ready-made cloths to be worn. Life was so very easy for the Santals. One morning, after smearing the raja's house walls with cow-dung, his servant girl went to the field to dump the refuse she collected. And there she sat for her call of nature. Sitting by the side of a rice-field with her hands unwashed, she plucked a few ears of rice. Seeing the girl polluting the rice, the creator God ordered husk to cover the rice and cotton-plants produce cotton alone. Since that day, the life of Santals became very difficult.

The barter system of economy is still prevalent in Santal villages today, though it has diminished very much. Money value has taken the place of the barter system in Santal society. The oppressive pyramidal economic structure that is based on currency value has concealed the tribal 'circular economic system'. As the Santals are not used to money and as they do not realize the value of money, they remain a prey to the exploitation of the Hindu merchants, moneylenders and government officials.

The econmic situation of the Santals can be described as 'consume now', i.e., living the present in full manner. The future by and large does not bother the Santals. Saving for a better future is not an accepted principle among them. They eat and drink and make merry when they have and go hungry when they do not have. The Santals call the summer as 'rengeć din,' for they finish-off all the food grains by the beginning of summer and will have nothing to eat during the summer. The economic backwardness has accentuated the isolation of the tribe very much. The inadequate health facilitics coupled with poverty has made the Santal population easy victims of disease and pestilence.

SOCIAL LIFE OF THE SANTALS

The tribe's collective and co-operative experiences of migration from Chae-Champa and settlement in the Damin-i-koh set the horizon to the earlier trends in Santal society.

For the Santals, the world is a vast arena in which man/woman, spirits and impersonal powers are constantly in touch with each other. The entire world is refered to as 'Towa-dare', the milk tree. Every house-hold, clan, sub-clan and village community must ensure its integrity and maintain the harmony.

Their's is a collective personality with the strongest sense of belonging to her/his clan or community and, she/he has her/his identity in so far as she/he is an integral part of the network of 'sagai', the Santal pattern of relationships. It is a very special cohesiveness among the Santals. The constituting factors are common origin and ancestory, common heritage and history, and common language and customs. 'Peṛa hoṛok'' and 'Peṛa beohar', exchange of visits and gifts respectively, enhance such a relationship. From birth to death, at every important stage of a Santal's life the entire village community and relatives participate. The whole community is at work, whether it is ploughing or transplanting; even hunting 'sendra' is a community activity. Their strong community dimension denotes that their's is a socialistic society antipodean to capitalistic society that is individualistic.

These trends gradually have come under much pressure by the increasing non-tribal presence and by the various efforts made by the Indian Government in particular to get them into the "national-mainstream" of life. This, today more than ever, is jeopardizing the social integrity of the Santals.

SOCIAL PROBLEMS OF SANTALS IN SANTAL HOME-LAND

Social problems of Santals in Santal home-land include : lack of schooling and adult education; great poverty and, in some areas seasonal hunger use, exploitation at weekly market by non-tribals, drunkennesss indebtedness and mortgaging of land to non-tribal money lenders unutilized man power during the agricultural season, inefficient agricultural practices land-holding fragmentation inadequate irrigation lack of access to forest resources scarcity of income generating activities lack of technical and managerial skills; and brain-drain of educated Santals.

Education

The literacy rate in Santal Parganas is 15.64%, 24.64% for males, 6.26% for females. The Government runs schools for children and adult education centres in the villages, but these are not well attended and the teachers themselves lack interest and motivation. Besides, very little has been done to conscientize the villagers on the need and importance of education. As per news paper reporting (Hindustan Times Nov. 17 'Primary Education off rails in Dumka'), nearly 207 primary and middle schools in the districts out of 1676 do not have their own buildings. Nearly 145 primary schools are closed owing to non-availability of teachers. Only 3689 teachers are working in different schools of the districts as against a sanctioned strength of 4487 units.

Adult education centres are mostly on paper. Under the 20-Points Programme the scheme was launched to literate the masses in the country to impart education to 50,000 persons in the state of Bihar. Minors ranging from 9 years to 14 years are also supposed to get non-formal education from this year.

Medical Facilities

The medical facilities in the area are very poor. There are 6 Government hospitals with a total of 468 beds. This gives one bed for every 2000. There are also reportedly, 41 Primary Health Centres, each with 6 subcentres. In many cases, however, these centres are still being built and the medical staff are not available. As per newspaper report (Search Light 10.3. '86. p.5 'Sub-standard medicine kills women') a woman died in Dumka after being given an injection of sub-standard quality during a family welfare operation. 'Requil' and 'Mamalgin' were used in these operations instead of the standard medicines, 'Sequil' and 'Analgin'. A huge quantity of sub-standard medicine has been purchased by the local Health Department Authorities.

Health-related Problems of Santals

The Santals attribute illhealth and disease to evil spirits. Unaware of the real causes of illness, the tribals are at the mercy of the 'Ojha'—witch-doctors who placate the spirits on payment of substantial fees. To pay the fees to the Ojha, people very often have to borrow money or mortgage their land. All illness of an individual thus becomes a calamity dragging the whole family into poverty. As regards child-birth practices, each village has its own 'dạị' who is called to attend the delivery. But it is done in a very unscientific and unhygienic way, often harmful and fatal. Some the most common diseases and health problems of the Santals are, T.B., Leprosy, high infant mortality, diarrhoea, disentry, malaria, skin-diseases, malnutrition, etc., Kala-azar is epidemic in the villages close to the Ganges.

Condition of Women

The condition of the women in India as a whole is pitiful. The society is patriarchal, patrilocal and patrilineal. In this socio-cultural frame-work women have always been discriminated against. The inequalities inherent in the Indian social system based on caste, community and class have aggravated the disadvantages of women of underprivileged groups, and also, whatever the caste or class a woman may belong to she is considered inferior in status, position and power relation vis-ā-vis of our group. Development has, in this developing country, worked against women's interests. Recent researches and surveys indicate that modern agriculture, industry and trade are keeping out women. Socially, women are still denied the recognition due to them. People to date react differently to the birth of a boy to that of a girl; in poverty stricken families nutrition and health care are concentrated on a boy while a girl is neglected; a school going boy receives encouragement from the family, while the school-girl in between school-hours is called upon to help her mother or grandmother in cooking, cleaning and looking after younger brothers and sisters; a boy is framed to the economically productive and develops the "masculine" virtues. While a girl is socialized in a sex-linked role and to imbibe "feminine" qualities. When married a woman is still subordinate to her husband and submissive to the in-laws. Wife-beating is common, dowry-death recurrent (in India during January-June 1982 totalled over 5,000 deaths) and demands for dowry on the increase, while cases of widow-remarriage are scant. There is a steady decline in sex-ratio of females per male. Among the Santals dowry problems don't exist but divorce is becoming common. However, it is to be noted that a woman in Santal society is given every right and privilege to move for divorce from her husband if he is allegedly involved in extra marital relations or for any other mal-adjustment in their conjugal life. The decree is given to the wife and she is permitted to remarry elsewhere. In any case, the Santals believe that inspite of their being divorced in this world they will meet again in the world to come.

Communication

Communication facilities in Santal Prganas are limited. The Railway Administration has reportedly treated Santal Parganas with a bias ignoring its legitimate claim. The entire division has only 219 kms. of railway tracks. 113 on the main line and 106 on the loopline. This construction was done between 1860 and 1882. After that not an inch has been added to what was constructed over a century ago. Dumka, the Divisional Headquarter has not been linked with railways though a proposal to link Dumka with Rampurhat is hanging fire for over three decades. Of the four districts in the division, only Deoghar and Sahibganj have railways. The nearest railway stations from the remaining two district headquarters, Godda and Dumka are located 14 to 30 kms. away. This results in a large quantity of agricultural products, vegetables, minerals, sabai grass, boulders, stone-chips etc not being able to go to big markets where they could fetch good prices. One of the most important reasons of backwardness of this region, predominantly inhabited by Santals is the absence of the railways.

In the matter of roads also the sprawling division is quite poor. Dumka district has only 500 kms. of road. It has no big industry. The only flourishing industry is that of silk which is concentrated in the hands of a few traders. It has a mumber of places famous for scenic beauties which can be developed into tourist spots. But these have not been brought into line light for want of communication.

Government and private bus services are irregular and inadequate. Cycle-rickshaws are found in townlets. Interior villages can be reached only by bullock-carts, bicycles, private jeeps or on foot. Postal services are erratic; telephone services exist only within the district headquarters.

SANTAL RELIGION

The Religious system of the Santal society that gives meaning to the behavioural pattern of the Santals is in turn greatly affected and subsequently it under-goes a lot of changes. Religion today, as Karl Marx said, has become an 'opium of the people; and the Santals are no exemption. God is being more alienated form the people. Ritual practices eliminate justice and righteousness. Men are intoxicated with such meaningless ritual practices that they even have become a "burden" to the Supreme-Being. This only leads to doom and destruction; and that exactly is the case with the Santals.

The Santals believe in monotheism. Thakurjiu is their God Supreme. He has a court of super-natural spirits called 'boṅgas' to help him. The court consists of a hundred and seventy 'boṅgas' classified into ten minor categories. These minor ones are regrouped into three major categories; viz:

(*i*) The Spirit of the dead ancestors,

(*ii*) The house-hold and tutelary spirits; and

(*iii*) Spirits known as village deities.

According to another traditional account, the Supreme God of the Santals is said to be 'Sing Boṅga' and his entire court is divided into six categories and are headed by the following 'boṅgas': Jaisim-Boṅga, Maraṅ Buru, Mõrẽko, Gossaiń era, Pargana-Buru and Mańjhi-haṛam Boṅga. However, the Supreme-Being is popularly addressed as 'Chando-Baba'.

The Santals believe that their world is inhabited by a large number of spiritual beings of various kinds called 'Boṅgas'. The 'boṅgas occupy the central place in the religious consciousness of the Santals. Therefore, the Santals are pre-occupied with the duty towards the 'boṅgas' and believe that only by coming to terms with 'boṅgas' can they be happy and free from diseases and disasters.

For the Santals, the world is a vast arena in which man, spirits and impersonal powers are constantly in touch with each other. Their religion, therefore, consists in entering into relationship with super-natural powers and spirits. It is important to foster friendly relationship with the 'boṅgas'. Every house-hold, sub-clan and village community must cultivate good relationship with the 'boṅgas' through supplications, rice-beer offerings, animal sacrifices and ceremonial sharing of sacrificial food, besides certain special observances and taboos. Their religious rites express, firstly, the conviction that the super-natural powers can be exercised by the 'boṅgas', and secondly the 'boṅgas' is invoked to secure the good will of the beneficient ones. Rites and rituals of the Santals signify the need of establishing an alliance with the benevolent 'boṅgas' and through them control the harmful ones. Reverential fear, dependence, submission and propitiation are the marks of the Santal's relationship with the Super-natural powers so that they can have land, cattle and children which are the prime cocerns of the Santals.

Sacrifice is something that is devoted to a deity and consumed either in his honour or by him alone, or by him and his worshippers. In order to honour the 'boṅgas' of their sub-clan, the Santals ensure their continuing care. Each house-holder sacrifices a pig (symbolizing a girl of the tribe) at the harvest festival of 'Sohrae'. Whenever rice-beer is drunk, a little of it is spilt on the ground for 'Maraṅ-Buru'. Whenever a meal is taken, a small portion is set aside for the 'oṛak' boṅga, and for the immediate ancestors. Everything good proceeds from good 'boṅgas' and they are honoured with sarifices. The evil 'boṅgas' are placated, lest they become angry and bring about vengeance. Listening to the Santal folk-lores, one is given to understand that the Santals at one time used to offer human sacrifices to water deities and earth deities. This practice is not in vogue in Santal Parganas today. In the former case, whenever a tank was dug and no water came out of it, the Santals ascribed the non-appearance of water to the wrath of the offended deity. They therefore, appeased him by drowning a human victim in the tank: A pole is planted at the centre of the tank, and then a man is tied to the pole. As the water level rose, the victim got drowned.

In the latter case, they used to kill a human victim and burry his corpse in the earth believing that the offended earth deity would be propitiated thereby and would confer good luck upon the offerer of the sacrifice.

Throughout the year the Santals are thus pre-occupied with pleasing and placating the 'boṅgas', and their destiny is understood to be solely dependent upon them. The fore-going practices were handed down to the present generation by their ancestors and are in vogue today. Beneath these practices undoubtably lies the fear of 'boṅgas' that choke every man of the tribe that is caused by his ignorance.

Besides these, the Santals are haunted by a deep rooted dread of witch-craft. It is the art of manipulating the malevolent 'boṅgas' to bring destruction upon one's enemy. Witches are exclusively feminine. Santals do not tolerate any witch among them. If a witch is caught, she is thoroughly bashed or hanged to death. There are folk-tales as to the origin of witch, the most typical of which is the following one :

As the folk-tales go, their ancestors one day went up to 'Maraṅ Buru' requesting him to give them a charm by which they could teach a lesson to their garrulous wives. He consented to their request and asked them to inscribe incantations on leaves with their blood. As it was evening, they were afraid of loosing their virility, and so they took leave of the 'Maraṅ Buru' to return on the following day. This was secretly watched by their wives. So, when the men returned home, they entertained them with delicious food and drink. Having pleased with the treatment, the men decided not to pursue their effort to learn the charm. The women repeated the treatment on the following day. While their husbands were dead drunk, they approached 'Marañ-Buru' in the guise of men and asked for incantation. 'Marañ-Buru' then initiated them as witches. Seeing their husbands snoring in their return, they began rebuking them by names. Infuriated by the rebuke of their wives, the men made their way to 'Marañ-Buru. He was taken-a-back and was annoyed at the foolery of the womenfolk. So, in order to counter-act the evil influence of 'Dạn', he taught them the way to become a 'Jaṇ' and 'Ojha'.

The Santals were and are so haunted by their belief in witch-craft that all the negative aspects of their inter-personal relations, diseases and even murders were and are interpreted as caused by the malign activities of the witches.

In sickness, the Santals go to 'Ojha' for cure. The 'Ojha' diagnoses the cause of the sickness by applying sacred oil on sal leaf. If he fails to restore the health of the ailing person, the help of 'Janguru' is sought. And 'Janguru' denounces the witch who is believed to be causing that sickness. Witch-craft as we see does not act as social restraint against aggression. Neverthe-less, aggression acts here in the limited sense; i.e., it is directed against women alone. So, it apprears as if the social root beneath witch-craft rests in the social constrainst against women only.

SOCIAL CELEBRATIONS

The Santals by nature are communitarian. Their village settlements stand a proof to their deep sense of belonging to a community. All normal activities of life and all the rites of passage necessitate the participation of the community. These celebrations, we must recall, are deeply rooted in the Santal tradition. This is evidenced in the popular Santali saying:

"Cithri huṭup′ danḍire hapṛamko duṛup′ kate achạr-bichạr ledako; kero ḍạḍi dak′ko ńu ańjeṭleda ar baṛe buṭạ ot hõ ko duṛup′ gaḍaleda" (their ancestors sat at hardy ground of Cithri huṭup′ to discuss and to finalize their age long customs; they sat there and discussed for so long a period and at one streach that the great kero spring got dried up quenching their thirst and the land under the peepul tree on which they sat became a ditch as if it were a pond). It was after such discussions did their ancestor handed-over such customs to their children and children's children. That's precisely why the Santals hold their culture and customs close to their hearts.

Rites of Passage

Rites and rituals at the critical stages of the life-cycle of a Santal indicate her/his close association with her/his own tribal community and with the spirit-world. Birth, initation, marriage and death are the significant stages that mark the life of an individual Santal. These crucial moments are triggered off by elaborate socio-religious rites and rituals. These rituals involve the blessings of the benevolent 'boṅgas' and also keep up the world of ideas regarding popullation and purification of the tribe.

Bathing, washing of hands and legs, shaving and fire are some of the popular symbols used by the Santals to remove impurity. 'Danḍom' is also a means of cleanliness used in other cases, not in rites of passage.

Janam Chaṭiạr

Relationship with ancestors and tribe, purification, and celebration are the tripple intrinsic values that are highlighted in the elaborate ritual of 'Janam Chaṭiạr'. Thogh it consists of the ceremonies held on 'janam hilok" and of the 'Nartha hilok", it specially has come to mean the latter.

For the Santals, child-birth is a defilement. The mother and child, the house and the village are considered defiled by the birth of a child. This idea of defilement no doubt points to the inter-wovenness of the social structure of the Santal community. Janam-Chaṭiaṛ ceremony therefore, purifies these defilements. Besides, it gives a name to the new-born babe admitting it into its father's spirits, for the Santal, world is closely linked-up with the supper-natural realm. The ceremony thus incorporates the child into the tribe.

Though the rituals like 'Bohao', 'Dora' and 'Sathe dak' are of prime importance, the 'Nim dak' manḍi' ceremony takes the prominance in 'Janam-Chaṭiaṛ'. A handful of margoza leaves are boiled along with rice powder and a bit of sugar is added to it. These symbolize hardship, sacredness and happiness accordingly of this earthly life, the race in which the child has just entered. Margoza leaf as we all know is medicinal, and so it too could be said to symbolize purification. The head of the household offers a bit of 'nim dak' manḍi' to 'Maraṅ-Buru' and to the ancestral spirits. It is an expression of the tribal community's gratitude to their God and to their ancestors for the child, and also invoking their blessings of the child. Besides, it is to remind themselves of the command given to the 'pilchu-Haṛam' and 'Pilchu-Buṛhi' by 'Liṭa' before they lay togeter as husband and wife. By sharing the 'nim dak' manḍi', the entire village is cleansed of the defilement. Therefore, this ceremony is popularly known today as "Nim dak' manḍi".

The cultural oppression by the surrounding dominant cultures has destroyed the Santhal culture to a very large extent and have left the Santals with a distorted form of 'Nim dak' manḍi' celebrations. Also the Christian missionaries to some extent have instilled in the Santals a feeling of aversion to their traditional ceremonies of 'Janam Chaṭiaṛ'. Their introduction of the Roman baptismal rite has contributed not only to the destruction of their sentimental customs handed over by their ancestors, but also to the prevailing ethnic alienation.

In case of a boy child, the purificatory ceremony is held five days after birth; And if a girl, three days after birth. This is not however, always observed. During the agricultural season, the boy child is taken through this in three days or even on the day of birth itself. This indicates the tough physic and the commendable satmina of a Santal mother. She can get into the field of action even a day after she gives birth.

The Santals in general have a firm belief in superstitions. A child must be taken through this ceremony inside the same lunar month in which it is born. They believe that the child born and not taken through the 'Chaṭiạr' inside the same lunar month would become a 'jom-hem'.

One may ask, what happens if the child is born on the day of the change of the moon? The Santals of course, have anticipated such quests. In such cases, a simple ceremony is performed by the mid-wife soon after the child birth. See takes the child out and puts it down on the dung-heap and sweeps the child-up on a winnowing fan with a broom and brings back the child as if it were a found child. Therefore, the child is not considered a new-born babe and so the entire village remains undefiled. The same is done incase a child is bron during festive time. This pretention of course is the denial of the reality of the child's birth. Such pretentions are not uncommon in the life of Santals.

CACO-CHATIAR: 'Caco' in Santali means 'toddling'. 'Caco-Chaṭiạr' is a ceremony by which a Santal male is taken into society.

The rite of 'Coco-Chaṭiạr' does not apply to Santal women, for they, being circumscribed from full participation in communal worship of the "national" deities and from eating the sacrificial meat can never be full-fledged members of Santal society. This ceremony till of late marked the second critical stage in the life-cycle of a Santal. This makes an individual a full-fledged member of the tribe giving the person the full rights of a Santal. This is the sacramental way of expressing acceptance of the young man as full participant in the village affairs. Traditionally, no Santal (male) could get married or burried until and unless the person underwent this initiation ceremony.

The highlight of this ceremony is the recitation of 'jiweť karam binti' — the Santal traditional history by a 'guru'. The 'guru' recites the tradition commencing with the creation of the world and finishing off with the elaborate description of how the tribe has come to the present abode, how the parents of the person were married and the person was born. In this way the person is brought into Santal history. Then the 'guru' entering into dialogue with the villagers present emphasizes the fact that the person has been purified of all his impurities, and that their drinking of 'hanḍi' is an expression of their willingness to accept the boy as a full pledged participant in their community affairs.

This beautiful ceremony by and large has been nullified in the Santal society today. Three major reasons that can be sighted for such nullification are :

(i) It is an expensive ceremony. The entire village community participates in the ceremony. And everyone is given 'sunum' and 'sasaṅ' to anoint oneself and treated with rice-beer. This of course many Santals could not afford ;

(ii) The dominant 'diku' cultures have instilled in the Santals a negative feeling towards it; and

(iii) The ignoring of the custom by Christian Churches. The Christian Churches re-placed 'Caco-Chạtiạr' with an uninculturated sacramental rite of confirmation. The Christians therefore, were left with no choice of practising their customary 'Caco-Chaṭiar'. This in turn has influenced the non-christian Santals. And so, Caco-Chaṭiaṛ' is a dead custom in Santal society today.

BAP'LA

Santal marriage is for eternity, for it continues even in 'hanapuri'. Balea+Balea=Bap'la. Etymologically, it is bringing together or uniting two clans or sub-clans of the tirbe. It is as much a union of two villages and two families as it is of two persons. It is a sacrament of vocation and commitment. A Santal marriagc takes place in the presence of a community, for it is an act that profoundly affects the Santal society. The young couple is supported and encouraged by the community as they pledge the gift of themselves to one another. This self-giving act indeed challenges and inspires all who partake in the ceremony.

The marriage rites make the Santal couple reproductive members of their community. It links the couple to the spirit world of the Santals. The use of water and 'sindur' at marriage manifest the element of purification and couple's access to their ancestoral spirits.

As a rule, Santal marriage is monogamous. Polygamy is favoured only in case of a barren wife and with her consent alone. Adult marriage is the accepted norm among Santals. They get their sons and daughters married at the age varying between eighteen to twenty-five years; and fourteen to eighteen years respectively. To preserve their tribal solidarity, they have stringent laws. Marriage of a Santal with someone of the same clan is a grave offence against the community, for the members belonging to the same clan are considered brothers and sisters in Santal society. Therefore, it is unlawful for a brother/sister to get married to his/her brother/sister. However, the tradition provides for either of the partner to change his/her title and get married in extreme cases. There is a large number of marriage forms is Santal society to ensure the non-violation of the endogamy and exogamy rules. However, all forms of marriage do not bear the same degree of social validity. As a rule, a Santal cannot marry a non-Santal, particularly, the 'dikus', for it involves a Santal womb. Those who breached this law are severely punished and are even excommunicated from the tribe. But as the Santal sanctions could not cope with the growing exploitative situation of the modern world, this rule has been relaxed vere much.

There are as many as eleven recognized forms of marriage among Santals : Kiriń bạhu se Sadhại bap'la—A bought bride marriage, Golãete bap'la—Inter marriage between two families in place of giving bride price, Tuṅki Dipil bap'la—marriage at groom's place by the bride carrying gifts in a basket to grooms' house, Saṅgha bap'la se Rạnḍi Chạḍwikowak' bapl'a—marriage between a widow and widower, Jãwãe kirińok' bap'la—marriage by giving groom price, Hirạm cetan ba'pla—marriage of a second wife, or ader bap'la—marriage by a boy forcefully taking a girl into his house to be his wife, N'ir bolok' bap'la—marriage by a girl forcefully getting into a boy's house as his wife, Iputuť bap'la—forced marriage by applying vermilion on the forehead of a girl, Apaṅgir bap'la—marriage of the boy and girl woh had illegal love affair, and Munḍu se Kunḍal ńapam bap'la—marriage by illicit connection.

Forced application of 'Sindur' on a virgin's forehead was an evil practice in Santal society and it derogated the dignity of grown up girls. However, it is to be noted that if a boy puts 'sindur' on the fore-head of a girl compulsively, and if the girl does not want to marry him, he is punished according to the custom. However, inspit of the 'ḍanḍom' that is meeted out to him, the girl cannot have a 'sadhại bap'la', for she is considered a 'chạḍwi'. But this being not so with the boy is a clear indication of unjudiciousness in Santal society.

Among all the forms of marriage that which is most prevalent among the Santals today is the 'kiriń bạhu bap'la se

Sadhạ̣i bap'la—the marriage of the bought bride or full dress wedding. This form of marriage bears the highest degree of social validity.

The entire event of Santal marriage can be divided into ten major parts :

(i) *n'epel* :

Having got the 'Raebarić' fix a girl for a boy, an arrangement is made for them to see each other face to-face along wiih their Parents and relatives. The venue for it is normally a public place like a fair or a market place or an open field. If both the parties are happy and satisfied, dates are fixed to visit each other's house along with their village 'Jog-mạńjhi'.

(ii) *Oṛak' duar n'el* :

This is popularly known as 'Taben jom'. The girl's father along with his relatives and the 'mạńjhi' of his village visit the house of the boy's village acts as an inter-mediary between the two parties. After the usual ceremonial greetings which includes the washing and anointing of feet, rice-beer is served to all the guests. After this the girl's party is shown the house, field and cattle of the boy. Then they discuss in details the bride-price which is called 'Gonoṅ'.

(iii) *Horok' Cikhna* :

This consists of two parts : 'Jãwãe Dhuti' and Bạhu Bande'. The 'raebarić' takes the girl's father, her uncle and all the village officials to the boy's house. The officials of the boy's village receive and escort them to the boy's house. Having exchanged greetings, their feet are washed and anointed with oil (it is a symbol of Santal acceptance and hospitality. It also symbolizes the alleviation of all possible evil influences which might have been gathered on their way.) Then the ceremonial giving of 'dhuti' takes place. The boy's party then in return go to the girl's house for 'bạhu bande'. The saree that is commonly used to drape the bride on the occassion of her marriage is a white one made into yellow by dipping in 'sanañ dak'' signifying solemenity and purification. (But the Churches have imported their whiteness in the place of the yellow saree).

(iv) *Taka Cal* :

It is a ceremonial giving of bride-price. They payment of money according to Santal is a proof of legal possession of the bride. In Santal society, it is the boy's Parents who pay for the bride; and so, the mounting crimes capitalizing on dowry that are prevalent in the nation-main-stream of social structure is not a phenomenon in Santal society. However, one cannot rule out the influence of the national-mainsteam in Santal society in trying to reverse the bride-price.

(v) *Gira Tol* :

It is a date fixing ceremony. The actual date of marriage is fixed through non-verbal communication, i.e., through visible signs and symbols. They use non-verbal communication lest the 'boṅgas' and the neighbours may hear of it and bring evil upon the couple and their house-hold.

(vi) *Manḍwa* :

It is the 'jog mạṅjhi' who gets the 'manḍwa' set. 'Manḍwa' is set-up both in boy's and girl's houses. It signifies the village co-operation in the wedding ceremony. It has a deeper meaning too. By setting-up of 'manḍwa', symbolically the very sacred-grove which is the dwelling place of the Supreme-Being and the ancestral spirits is brought into the court-yard of the house. They are brought in to bless, to participate and to enjoy themselves with the entire community. The 'tala-khunṭi' which is at the centre of the 'Manḍwa' symbolizes the Supreme Being as the centre of the marriage contract and of the whole marriage ceremony. The foot of the 'tala khunṭi' is covered with a mound of mud with carbon drawings of 'Tharwa' on it symbolizing evil (cf. Dak' dap'la myth). On the 'dak' bap'la' day morning, this is symbolically sanctified by giving a coating to it with holoṅ dak'.

(vii) *sunum sasaṅ ojok* :

It is the anointing of the people who assemble beneath the 'manḍwa' with oil and turmeric and are given 'hanḍi' to drink. This is more in line of purification. (It is to be recalled, from the day of 'manḍwa' both the bride and the groom are given 'sunum sasaṅ ojok' thrice a day for three days, that is, until the day of marriage). This is followed by 'dak' bap'la' and "Tarwardi bap'la' (appendix 2 and 3). Many writers describe these as exclusively a fertility cult. But in reality, it is quite contrary to their conclusions. Both 'dak' bap'la' and 'Tarwardi bap'la' depict the people's triumph over evil and are rooted in their twin myth. Another outstanding feature of it is the reminiscence of a loving kinship with the Supreme-Being and their ancestral spirits. The tying of the arrows at the 'dak' ghat' with white thread is symbolic of that bond of kinship. Thus, this elaborate ceremony manifests the hearty wishes of the community for the young couple. This is followed by a ritual called 'siṇan' in which 'baṛsi sutam' takes its prominance.

(viii) *Baṛiatok'* :

From the social point of view, 'bariaṭok'' is the most important marriage ceremony. The 'jogmaṇ̇jhi' of the bride's village along with the entire village community receives the groom and the groom's party at the outskirt of the village and 'daram dak'' ritual is conducted. 'Balea johar' that signifies the social bond entered into by the two families takes place. The groom is taken on a palanquin from house to house with song and dance (The traditional 'natwar dhon' is significant in this ceremony). This is an indication of the solidarity of the bride's village community. At this ceremony the groom pays a special respect and reverance to the 'mạńjhi' at the 'mạńjhi than' of the village.

Once all these are over, the preliminary ceremony to the 'sindradan' takes place at the 'chaṭka'. The younger brother of the bride is dressed up; he and the groom are lifted up on the shoulders facing each other and a white dhoti is held in between to divide them. Both the in-laws sprinkle water at each other and then they feed each other with 'adwa caole'. This is considered auspicious and purificatory.

(ix) *Sindradan* :

This is a symbolic ceremony to seal the marriage bond. It is to be noted that the bride and the groom fast the whole day until this ceremony as a purificatory measure. The girl is brought to the 'chaṭka' raised aloft on a 'dauṛa'. She covering her head with her saree tightly, sprinkles the mixture of coins and 'adwa caole' on the pepole gathered. Once the groom is lifted on the 'rahi' and brought face to face with her, they sprinkle water over each other. Having done that the groom tries to uncover the bride's face. With much difficulty when he succeeds, he using his right-hand-thum and the little finger, applies 'sindur' on the fore-head on the partition of her hairs thrice and then he smears her fore-head with rest of the 'sindur' along with the leaf. After that he takes her from the 'dauṛa' to himself into the 'rahi' and then two corners of their clothes are tied together symbolizing their oneness.

The use of vermilion (though originally, the Santals were using red mud) is very significant. It may be argued that the Santals borrowed the use of this particular ingredient 'sindur' from the Hindus. But as the tradition goes it was the Hindus who borrowed this trait form the aboriginal tribes and in course of time discovered sindur as a convenient red ingredient to be used for the purpose. And this synthetic red ingredient was borrowed by the Santals. Vermilion symbolizes life and sacrifice. The applying of a 'sindur' gives the bride the complete status of fully married wife. The use of 'sindur' in Santal society has a deeper meaning in relation to the 'boṅgas'. It makes a person to have access to the 'boṅgas'. Till the 'sindradan' the bride keeps in touch with her father's 'boṅgas'. This is re-placed by her husband's 'boṅgas' from the time of the 'sindradan' and will have no access to her father's 'boṅgas' anymore.

(x) *Giḍi Cumaura* :

It is a departure ceremony. It is also known as 'kanṭhar buṭa' (appendix—4). It begins with the addresses of the head-men of both the party's villages. The union and relationship between both the villages as a result of the marriage is emphasized in their addresses. The waving ceremony that is very impressive is the one that takes place in the groom's house: The mother-in-law washes and anoints the face of the bride, feeds her and kisses her as an expression of her deep love and acceptance. And the bride in turn does the same. Then the bride is asked to serve the guests. By this the bride is made to feel at home and helped in getting her acquainted with the village community and relatives. Then an address is made by the groom and the bride. To this, the bride responds to the officials and the people present to the effect, as all these have been brought about by the Supreme-Being, and Supreme-Being has joined them together and they have witnessed it; that they would remain faithfull to the marriage union with one another as husband and wife and would treat her in-laws as her own Parents. Finally, the brother of the bride gives her some insturction. And with the exchange of final greetings, the entire marriage ceremony winds up.

The most significant ritual in the entre marriage ceremony is the 'hanḍi codor' at the 'maṇjhi than' that preceedes each ritual. Though it is a ritual of thanks-giving and invocation of blessing on the young couple, it primarily is a reminder of the larger family to which the Santals belong to.

It is a tragedy that a marriage ceremony so beautiful as this has been outrightly condemned as evil and been undermined by Christian Churches and disregarded by the dominant 'diku' cultures. Such disregard for the customs that are of great value to the Santals society is the worst type of crime that can be committed against them.

BANḌAN

In its broader sense 'banḍan' would comprise of 'Gok' sahan' and 'Jaṅbaha' ceremony, but in its stricter sense it is the last act of giving to the dead and asking the ancestors to keep him/her in their company.

The vaccum created by the death of a person in Santal society brings in an awareness of the occurence of a sudden sinister crisis in the village. Death indicates the victory of all the hostile 'boṅgas' over the benevolent major 'boṅgas'. Death brings in a momentary pollution in the village......the entire village is deprived of its tribal guardian spirits. The 'boṅga' of the dead man remain a source of menace to all in the village until the 'banḍan' ceremony. He is believed to remain in the clutches of the hostile 'boṅgas' till the fifth day of his death when the purification ceremony is performed. According to the means the relative of the dead person make a feast with rice-beer. A guru recites the 'mora karam binti'; as at the 'caco-chaṭiạr' the person was brought into life, now he has been taken out of life and into 'hanapuri'. An animal is sacrificed to him; water is libated to him and his/her 'boṅga' is invoked. Through this ceremony the village is safe-guarded against the evil influence of the 'boṅgas' and also the soul of the deceased is freed.

In case the 'boṅgas' of the 'hapṛamko' are soon forgotten or any conventional tribute to them is with-held, they likely visit the family with sickness, loss and worries. The recent dead must be given their due offerings at all important occassions. During the major festivals of the tribe, special sacrifices have to be made to the 'hapṛamko' until their names are lost to memory.

It is to be noted that until 'banḍan' is performed, the people of the house concerned do not libate 'handi', do not use 'sindur' and do not have any marriage. And the cancerned village do not hold any celebration.

For the Santals, 'banḍan' is very much associated with 'Nãe gada' (Damodar river) for it has its origin there. According to tradition, as their ancestors were crossing 'Ajoy gaḍa' after passing through 'siń duaṛ', one of them died. And when they reached 'nãe gada' they cut a bit of hair, hewed two nails from hands and one nail from the right leg of the dead man and pushed them together under the water ('um rakap' kedako') so as to enable him to walk along in the company of their ancestors who were in 'hanapuri'. Therefore, even today, the wish of a Santal is to go to 'nãe gaḍa' and take a dip atleast once in his/her life time.

FESTIVALS

Feasts and festivals are another major phenomenon in the social life of the Santals. Almost all the festivals are connected with agricultural and other activities of practical importance. Though the Santals have numerous feasts and festivals a around the year, I will be discussing only a few major festivals in this passage.

Erok' Sim

Erok' Sim means the sowing fowl. It is the first sacrifice offered to the benevolent 'boṅgas' in the Santal year. The feast falls in the Santal month of jhent-sar (May-June). The 'naeke' collects a fawl from every house-hold of the village and sacrifices them to the 'boṅgas' invoking their blessing for a good harvest. Besides this public sacrifice, there are also private sacrifices offered at homes for 'oṛak'-boṅgas', ancestral spirits and to the 'Maraṅ-Buru'. Drinking rice-beer, singing and dancing accompany this feast, for the Santals can have no feast devoid of these tripple elements.

Sohrae

Sohrae is the five day festival which a Santal longs to celebrate. As any other ethnic group, the Santals do celebrate their harvest festival in a grand scale. It is the Principal feast of the Santals as their principal food is rice. This feast is celebrated in the month of Pus (December-January). Unlike the other feasts, it involves much preparation—houses are renewed, new clothes are bought, plenty of rice-beer prepared and as many as possible kin and kith are invited for the celebration. The entire land of Santals bubbles with joy and gaiety on this festival. It is the festival of thanks giving—of love and brother-hood/sister-hood. The great freedom the Santals experience at this festival mentally takes them back to the golden-age of the tribe when they were in Chae-Champa.

Mag Sim

This is celebrated in the month of Mag (January-February). The final sacrifice to the ordinary national 'boṅgas' and to the 'simạ-boṅgas' is offered to mark the end of the Santal year. The special feature of this festival is the traditional resignation of all the village officials and the peoples' declaration to give-up their belongings. After every one present shared the rice-beer specially prepared for the occasion, the resignation is with-drawn and everyone resume their work as usual.

Baha Porob

It is the second great festival of the Santals celebrated in the month of Phagun (February-March). It is the Santal flower festival—a festival that marks the bloomings of 'maťkom' and 'sarjom' trees. As at this festival the Santal land is adorned with the flowers of these trees, the Santal new-year too blooms. This festival therefore, marks the commensing of the Santal new-year.

The people who stand in 'landa-sagai' relationship throw pure water at each other to merry themselves. The use o- 'sarjom Baha' and 'dak'' at this festival express certain sacredf ness about it.

The fore-going bird's eye-view of the traditional customs of some of the major events in Santal social life and reflection on the playing-down of those customs by the dominant 'diku' cultures and by the Churches in Santal home-land necessarily inculcates a sense of hatred towards the 'dikus' and dislikeness towads the institutional Churches. If the alienating spirit of the 'diku' cultures and of the Churches is not alienated, the time will soon come when both the 'dikus' and the Church will be alienated from the land of Santals in their entirety.

SANTAL CULTURE

Culture is a set pattern of values and way of life on an ethnic group. The cultural pattern, therefore, varies from group to group. The entire civilization of India is said to be based on cultures belonging to about 600,000 communities with a vast range of time behind. Santals are one of these major tribal ethnic groups.

A social group irrespective of its size possesses a set of beliefs, traditions, customs, and institutions which are implicity accepted by the group as relatively immutable and as conducive to their well being. This is true of the Santals.

The Santals call themselves 'hoṛ-hopon'. Literally it means 'sons of mankind'. However, it carries also the implicit meaning, 'the true-men'—the only really human society. The Santals, a colourful tribe of Santal-Parganas in Bihar have also spread into numerous districts in Bihar and its neigh-bouring states. There are different versions about the number of clans and their origin. Traditionally, the Santal society was divided into seven clans: Hansdak' Murmu, Kisku, Hembrom, Marandi, Soren and Ṭudu. The after-math of the deluge added five more clans: Baske, Besra (Bas+era), Bedea, Cõṛe and Pauria. Each clan has its cluster of sub-clans. The Hansdak' clan had forty-one sub-clans, Murmu sixty-five, Kisku thritytwo, Hembrom thirty-two, Marandi forty-nine. Soren forty-six, Ṭudu forty-eight, Baske thirty-one, Besra twenty-seven, Bedea one, Cõṛe eighteen and Pauria sixteen. Thus they have four-hundred and six sub-clans in all (appendix—5).

Santali is the language of the tribe. It can be classified as an Austric language akin to Mundari, Savara and other languages of the eastern sector of central India. Strictly speaking, Santali is a dialect even today. The Christian missionaries who came to this area during British rule introduced Roman script to it. Much of Santal literature is found today in this script. The Indian government, of late is trying to avert that script by introducing devnagiri script. In 1905 Pandit Raghunath Murmu brought out a script for Santali called 'Ol Chiki', the characters of which are still an issue of discussion. Thus the non-determination of Santali script has created a vacuum in the self identity of the Santals. This has led many educational institutions in Santal-Parganas to ignore the language. The tragedy therefore, is that the medium of education for the Santal students is not their mother-tongue, but Hindi a 'diku' language. So, discrimination like giving Santali not even a secondary status in the Santal home-land is highly resented. The influence of dominant ethnic groups around them have made the Santals bi-lingual. Either they are to know Santali and Hindi or they are to know Santali and Bengali. The Santal way of communicating their ideas and feelings to others is very figurative and ceremonial unlike their counterparts, the 'dikus'.

The traditional Santal dress is very simple and harmonious to the colour of nature. The men-folk wear 'Panji' and 'dạhṛi' and the women-folk 'panci' and 'parhat'. The cultural influence of the dominant ethnic groups has imported dhoti, banian, pants, shirt etc. for men; saree, blouse etc. for women into their culture. Such cultural influence is very strong in the towns of Santal-Parganas.

The Santal women love to adorn themselves with silver ornaments. Whenever a Santal woman goes out of her village especially to market places, she dresses neatly and adorns herself with all possible ornaments. Men in general do not use any ornament in these days. Santal women like Tamil women love adorning themselves with flowers.

Music and dance flow in the blood of the Santals. The Santals have 31 type of dances and 20 tunes to suit their life-cycle. They enjoy singing and dancing all through the night. It is an expression of their deep sense of community and of 'Rạskạ.' It is a sight to see the Santals singing and dancing. The Santal girls singing at work and as they return home from work, the Santal shepherd boys holding bamboo-flutes in hands, the sweet melody of the flutes that floats in the air of Santal villages are all expressions of that 'rạskạ'—their joyful attitude to life. Every Santal tale ends with the note of 'rạskạ' is characteristic of them.

The Santals are neat and clean. They keep their surroundings too very clean. It is a pleasure to see their huts with plastered and painted mud-walls. They are so sensitive about cleanliness that one could even call that a mania.

The Santals by nature are hardy. They are extremely good at reclaiming land. They are masters of the forests. They love exploring hills and forests with their axe, bows and arrows. They eat almost all kinds of birds and animals, both domestic and wild. Drinking and merry-making is part and parcel of their life.

Their transformation from pastoral to agrarian village community system came into being while they were at Chae-Champa. This was re-inforced when they settled down in the land called 'Saont'. As an agrarian society rice became their stable food. One distinct characteristic of Santal society is that it is an egalitarian society in which democratic norms prevail for taking decisions based on consensus. Every Santal has a say in the socio-cultural, political, economic and religious affair of the community. The group leadership is thus up-held in Santal society.

The Santals are generous, hospitable and possess a good will to share their wealth with other members of his/her community. The 'loṭa dak" they offer to their guests is always over-flowing is an expression of that. Though the radius of Santhal world is small, they have a world of 'peṛako'. Treating 'peṛa-hoṛ' with generous hospitality is a matter of joy for them. It is interesting to note that there are no orphans in Santal Society. It is a unique characteristic of the Santals that no member of the community feels isolated or secluded except in cxtreme cases where one is isolated from the community temporarily for some serrious reason.

In any society, it is the women who provide the basis for its cultural maintenance. It is the same with Santals too. Though the Santal society is partrilineal, by their active participation in almost all the activities of the family, the Santal house-wife has carved her prominancy in her family. Except for ploughing which tradition forbids, she actively participates in agricultural operations. Handling house-hold chorus is her pleasure. Besides her having a say in all matters concerning domestic and non-domestic matters, she is also invarriably consulted by her husband and children. Progenity is considered God's blessing for them. Therefore, active participation in sexual activities by man and wife are culturally favoured. The women-folk by convention do not take part in 'kulhi durup". They are also not permitted to take part in any religious sacrifice or eat of that sacrifice. This of course makes the Santal egalitarianism limping.

The Santals are very strict about the behaviour of their girls. Santal girls are not expected to be friend any 'diku'. If a girl is found being friendly with a 'diku' boy, the Santal boys would bring upon her much shame and humiliation by abusing her sexually. This is prevalent even today. It is in this regard, tattooing among Santal women has become very common. The colour is made by mixing charcoal with human milk. Needle and thorn are used to draw ornamental designs. According to their belief and religious tradition, tattooing is intimately connected with certain immemorial superstitions. Santal philosophy that regards death at the donor of endless life and beatitude, is believed to vest tattooing with power to propitiate a 'banga' or comfort a soul on its journey in 'hanapuri'.

According to another tradition, all the silver ornaments are taken away before a Santal woman is burried, but the only ornament that she takes with her to 'hanapuri' is the one that is inseparable from her body, that is the ornamental designs made by tattooing. Therefere, the Santal women love tattooing.

All these are a later understanding of tattooing; but originally, the Santal women were tattooed in order they be distinguised from non-Santal women and be easily recognized and rescued incase of sexual exploitation by the 'dikus',

With powerful ethnic groups pressing on all sides, the Santals today face a ceatain amount of a cultural identity crisis. The failure of the 'hul' (1855-57) contributed to the acculturation and assimilation of the dominant 'diku' cultures to a very great extent. The Santals have developed a feeling of 'rand concession synodrum' — an inferiority feeling in relation to other cultural groups. This is expressed in their repetition of "boka kanale".

A process of tribal disintegration is systematically at work. The increasing non-tribal presence in the areas is imposing itself on the life and culture, and the Santals are getting off their cultural roots and their precious home-land itself! In the long rnn, the tribals may become non-descript. The process of sanskritization is at the same time the process of de-tribalization socio-economically as well as religioculturally.

The principal elements that have been operating on the Santals' life since the nineteen century are Hinduism, and the British Government which is now re-placed by the Indian gevernment. These two elements have disintegrated and destroyed Santal culture extensively and subsequently, have brought in alien values in their life.

The Santals are a beautiful people enshrining in their life-style sublime values, such as co-operation, mutual obligation, community solidarity, the sense of equality between men and women and family harmony. India would be poorer without them. They cherish such cultural values as straightforwardness, sincerity, honesty, truthfulness. Destroy the Santals and you will destroy these values from the heart of this nation. The Santal society does not know caste-system and communal clashes; there is no dowry system and cases of dowry deaths. Female infanticide and bride-burning are unheard of among the Santals in India

It is alleged that at present some of the personnel of the various departments posted in Santal-Parganas are not only indifferent but possitively hostle towards the Santals. Some at the lower levels state that the Santals are 'jangalis', will never learn anything and the efforts of the government to 'civilize' them are bound to be futile.

Nehru's Tribal 'Panchesheel' reiterates : "People should develop along the lines of their own genius and should avoid impossing anything on them. We should try to encourage in every way their own traditional arts and culture" (appendix—I). Yet it often stated that the objective of the trible development is to enable the tribals to join the mainstream of the national life. What this mainstream, is, is anybody's guess. The tribals say, "Ours is the mainstream, you are welcome to join it." Let the non-tribals acquire some of the good and healthy traits of the tribal culture as the expect they latter to acquire their own.

THE POLITICAL LIFE OF THE SANTALS

As an effect of the Santal 'hul' (1855-57), an exclusive political territory was decided for the Santals under the name 'Santal-Parganas'. This land of the Santals is bounded on the north by Bhagal-pur and Purnea districts of the state of Bihar; in the east by Malda, Murshidabad and Birbhum districts of West-Bengal; the Bihar district of Dhanbad and the West-Bengal district of Burdwan in the south; and in the west by

Hazaribagh, Monghyr and Bhagalpur districts of Bihar. From the time of the Britishers till the year 1985 the entire land of Santal-Parganas stood under a single administrative unit having its head-quarter at Dumka. Of late, it has been divided into four administrative districts : Dumka, Sahibganj, Deoghar and Godda. By this division the identity of united Santal-Parganas has been lost and the name 'Santal-Parganas' has been subtly eliminated from the administrative usage of the government. And regrettably, of late, the Jesuits in Santal-Parganas too have done away with the name. This no doubt, positively contributes to the ethnic disintegration of the Santals.

Village is the basic unit of the political system of the Santals. They have their traditional administrative system and social institutions to look after village affairs. There is the village council headed by village headman called the 'mańjhi' and this council is represented by the elders of the village conversant with Santal customary laws and regulations based on tribal values and moral sensibilities. This Panchayat is responsible for framing rules for village administration, enforcement of customary rule for the common welfare and taking judicial action on persons for breach of customary rules and tribal conduct.

A full fledged village council consists of seven village officials : Mańjhi, Paranik, Naeke, Kudom-naeke, Jog-mańjhi, Jog-Paranik and Godeť. This port-folio is hereditary. However, it can be with-drawn by the villagers by concensus in case an official proves himself incompetent in his job.

Then there is the confederation of several called village 'Parha' or 'Pargana'. Its head, the Pargana who is assisted by a desh-mańjhi, is the strongest and the most influencial functionary of any village councils clustered together. This inter-village confederacy legislates for the common good of the villages under its control. The main characteristic of such a socio-political institution is that decisions are arrived by consensus and not by taking votes as is the procedure in modern democracy.

The leadership pattern in Santal society is collegial and not hierarchical. Anyone can be headman 'mańjhi', priest 'naeke' etc. if the community decides. If anything, the individual is reluctant to assume such authority. Moreover, any such authority is extremely accountable to and punishable by the group. It is really a different concept of leadership, a group leadership, which can result in an immensely effective process of group-decision-making within tribal limits. 'Kulhi Duṛup" is the community meetings where consensus is reached and is confirmed by the headman.

The next political unity of the Santals is the 'Pargana'. It is a cluster of villages under a headman known by that name assisted by a desh-mańjhi.

The Supreme national council of the Santals is the 'Lo Bir' which is presided over by the 'dihri'. The people in a special way are the highest authority in this council. The role of the officials in this council is to help the people arrive at dicisions on the matters of discussion. The administrative set-up of this hunt-council indicates the collective system by which the aboriginal Santals were guided. As we have seen a little earlier, at the feast of 'Mag Sim', the village officials resign their posts and the people in turn declare the surrender of their possessions to the village headman reveal the traces of communal system that once existed in Santal society.

The above councils invariably are vested with much judicial power. All cases are settled in their respective councils. If the intra-village disputes could not be settled-up by their respective 'mańjhis' the matter is referred to the 'Pargana' and if the 'Pargana' fails, it is taken-up by 'Lo Bir' council. Punishments for serious breaches of the tribal law such as 'biṫlaha' are exclusively decided by the hunt-council. It is to be noted that at the hunt-council, the 'Pargana' and other officials stand in equal footing with the ordinary people. They will have no authority vested on them. Whatever may the people decide under the guidance of the 'dihri' would stand. There is no appeal against its judgement. It is an administration of the people, by the people and for the people.

The Santals enjoy recalling the myth in relation to their whole set of political organization. It describes the mighty kingdom which the Santals once constituted. Each clan had a specific role to play : the Kiskus were kings, the Murmus priests, the Soren warriors etc. (This is not to be understood as the class-system or caste-system of Hinduism). This they consider was the golden-age of their history.

A separate chapter in the Constitution of India containing only one Article, i.e., Article 244, is devoted to the scheduled and Tribal Areas.

Pursuant to this Article, the fifth schedule to Constitution contains provisions regarding the administration and control of the scheduled Areas. Bihar is one of the 8 states having scheduled Areas.

Again, Nehru's Tribal 'Panchesheel' states :

> 3—We should train and build up a team of their own people to do the work of administration and development. Some technical personnel from outside will, no doubt, be needed especially in the begining.

But we should avoid introducing too many outsiders into tribal territory.

4—We should not over-administer these areas or overwhelm them with a multiplicity of schemes. We should rather work through, and not in rivalry to, their own social and cultural institutions.

5—We should judge results, not by statistics or the amount of money spent, but by the quality of human character that is evolved.

Despite all the above safe-guards, there has been a considerable change in the political life of the Santal community during the last 42 years. As there have been changes in the social order, the traditional authority system is losing its original role. The imposition of a democratic system designed for the more advanced regions of rural India has had the effect of undermining the old authority structure without replacing it with a practical alternative suitable to Santal society. The splitting up of well-knit villages and the formation of blocks from parts of different villages look like an almost deliberate attempt to undermine village cohesion, but probably due to bureaucraitc convenience without any regard to the diverse social effects.

BIHAR GOVERNMENT ADMINISTRATIVE DIVISIONS OF SANTAL—PARGANAS

Total number of Districts	...	4
Total number of sub-divisions	...	6
Total number of blocks	...	41
Total number of halkas	...	410
Total number of panchayats	...	770
Total number of towns		
(i) having population of 20,000 to 49,999		4
(ii) having population below 20,000		7
Total number of villages	...	12,174

POLITICAL MOVEMENTS OF THE SANTALS

The first and prominant movement in Santal history that gave vent to the deep aspiration of the Santals for freedom was the 'Santal-Hul'. It gathered-up momentum under the leadership of the twin brothers—'Sidu and Kanu' in the year 1855. The Santals dexterously fought their oppressors. But to their misfortune the bullets of the Britishers prevailed in the fight. After this defeat the Santals acknowledged that under prevailing conditions any increased political power and improvement in rank could not be abtained by military might. This recognition contributed to the decline of solidarity.

The year 1871 saw the rise of 'sapha hoṛ' movement. This movement that had the food habits of the Santals as its main concern had a religious trait in it. This movement was greatly influenced by Hinduism. Meat which the Santals feast on could not be eliminated from the Santal menu and so, this movement was quite unsuccessful among the Santals.

During the national movement for freedom in the year 1942, the Santals actively participated in it under the guidance of their own tribal leaders. When the condition was chaotic, the Santals burned down the Dak bungalow of Bokara bandh and looted government properties.

Disom-Sendra movement came into being in 1950. It was the movement against the oppression of the money-lenders and government officials. The oppressed Santals vowed to drive all the 'dikus' out of Santal-Patganas. They used both peaceful and violent methods to drive them out. As India had its own government by then, the government gave orders to arrest the Santals to quell their up-rising. The government wanting to appease the Santals,formed a peace-council consisting of prominant tribal leaders of various tribes. Subsequently, the tribal leaders formed a political party known as Jharkhand. Getting a separate province for the Santal and the other tribals around was the prime motive of this party. This aspiration of the party has been fanned once a while and now it is gathering momentum.

On the 19th of April 1986 a group of Santals living in Bhańjhi (Sahibganj District) rose against the Bhagats whose exploitation the Santals could not stomach. The two major causes for their standing up in arms were :

(i) The exploitation of the forest by the Bhagats for their self interest and laying the blame on the Santals for it before forest officials. This put many innocent Santals in trouble with the police; and

(ii) The alledged murder of a Santal by the Bhagats. This up-rising led to the planned police attrocity that left fourteen Santals including their prominant leader, a one time Member of Parliament Antony Murmu dead.

The Santals of Bhańjhi haven't yet recuperated from the police attrocity.

The political culture that is prevalent in Bihar as one realizes is conducive to a more efficient manipulation of the masses leading to eventual negation on their human dignity. This on the other hand contributes to the rising political consiousness of the masses. That in turn gives vent to numerous political movements.

Such movements are quite often viewed as subversive of existing political structure of authority. These struggles, however legitimate, are liable to be misconstrued as threats to law and order and even national security. In such situation even legitimate and simple democratic dissent may get stifled not only by the musclemen of landlords but also by the coercive agencies of State in the interest of stabitity and law and order. The hapless and helpless Santals naturally also in such circumstances tend to believe that some of their leaders are being manipulated by the party in power.

The government's intervention in the traditionally eglitartian socio-political set up is apt to have a chaotic effect. The power assumed by the Government, for example, to appoint village leaders and Parganas is considered by the Santals, as adversely affecting their socio-political structure.

AWAKE YOU SANTAL

Hihiṛi Pipiṛi sona dolan (2)
Okarem bagiada thonok gaṛ do (2)
Beṅgeṫ ruaṛme adiwasi boeha
Okare ḍhariakan (2) Santal somaj.

Doho menak'gea itihas do
Kạhni muthạn leka teheń do
Santal jati mabon ebhenok'ma
Ạkil horte boeha (2) taṛam lạgiṫ.

Uduk' akana sedae reak'
Moñj somaj dobon belakoa
Ayurko jemon lahaseć taṛam lạgiṫ
Ebhen bạisigeye (2) ạyurbonae.

—Courtesy : S.D.C., Dumka.

Translation :

Hihiri Pipiri wherein we had our golden palace
Where have you left all that glorious palace ?
Awaken you tribe and look back
Where have you hung-up Santal society ?

All is jotted down in history,
But it's just as a fairy-tale today.
Let we the pilgrim Santal awake
And walk in the path of knowledge.

The past is known to us
Let us build a new society
So, you leaders lead us on
In the light of 'Ebhen Bạisi'.

CHAPTER 3

The Santal Rebellion and Liberation Theology

It was among the Santal settlers in the Damin-i-koh that the rebellion of 1855, known as the 'Hul', had its origin. It is haleid by some historians as a precursor to India's first war of independence. The Santal 'Hul' was the volcanic erruption of the molten lava of thc Santals' aspiration to be free form the clutches of their oppressors. Three prominent reasons can be cited for the out-break of the 'Hul', viz :

(i) The fraudulent manipulation of the 'diku' money-lenders who falsified accounts, committed perjury in court-actions, and corrupted government clerks and police officers with bribes;

(ii) The rapacity of the tax-collectors and 'diku' landlords collecting land-taxes; and

(iii) The cruelty of the police.

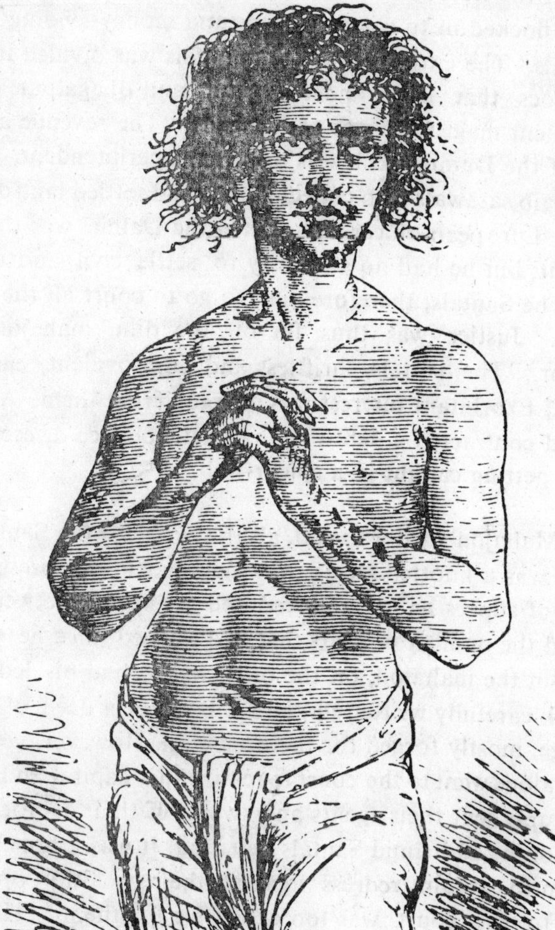

KAKU
A Man of Vision for the Santal Society

The above grievances are said to be due very largely to the absense of the European officials and the presence of the 'dikus' who had flocked in to carry on trade and money-lending among the Santals. The entire land of the Santals was divided into two major blocs that came under Birbhum and Bhagalpur; and the only resident magistrate was at Deoghar. The revenue administration of the Damin-i-koh was under a superintendent, assisted by four Saib sasawals who collected rent and settled land disputes. The only European officer who visited the Damin was the Superintendent; but he had no authority to settle civil and criminal cases. The Santals, therefore, had to go to court all the way to Deoghar. Justice was thus far off, the 'diku' mahajon was at their door. The Santals, thriftless and improvident, easily got into debt: Exorbitant interest was charged from them. And once they had contracted a debt they had little chance of escape. It was like getting caught in a spider-web.

If a Mahajon sued a Santal, all the evidence the Santal could produce was a knotted string (in which the knots represented the number of rupees he had received and the spaces between them indicated the number of years that had elapsed since he took the loan). But the mahajon, on the other hand, had his ledger and day-book carefully written-up, and a bond or a deed of sale or mortgage, mostly forged for the occassion. However, very rarely the mahajons went to the court to realize this capital and interest. They simply sent their agents and swept off their debtor's cattle. The ignorant and timid Santals felt thal it was a hopeless task for them to obtain redress against their wealthy oppressors. Going to the court was too expensive for them. They could never get justice, for the police and the administration played in the hands of the 'diku' money-lenders. Thus the government asserted its position neither through its executive machinary in the Damin-i-koh.

As cultivation extended, the 'dikus' induced the Santals to sell some of their surplus lands to them. Thus the 'dikus' gradually extended their holdings. They secured the best lands in the villages by exacting mortgages from the Santals in return for loans. And consequently, the Santals were driven to commerce life again by clearing fresh jungle and founding new villages only to be ousted by the 'diku' money-lenders.

The 'diku' mahajons and money lenders' execution of bonds played much mischief among the Santals. By bond, the debtor promised to work out his debt by personal service and the payment of an exorbitant rate of interest. Thus a Santal became a 'kamiya'. The remark made in this regard by Sir. William Le Fleming Robinson (a member of the British India Civil Service who in 1858 secured its abolition in Santal-Parganas) makes the reader's blood shoot-up :

> "I have had a bound brought to me in which Rs. 25/- was originally borrowed by a man (Santal) who worked his life time, his son did ditto, and I released his grandson from any further necessity; it had been running on for over thirty years, if I remember rightly !"[2]

Here is an extract from the statement made by Kanu Santal on the 20th of December 1855, to show how the police played in the hands of the 'diku' mahajons and money-lenders against the innocent Santals : complained to Buru Daroga that Sidu and Kanu were collecting men to commit a dacoity.

> "...The mahajons gave him Rs. 100/- to come and catch us. The Daroga, sitting at Babupaṛa sent his peon to me. He counted my men. Then I sent a note through him to the Daroga saying, the Thakurjiu has descended and we have assesmbled with the purpose of making a complaint to him;

so do not interfere......Then he (the Daroga) said, "You are collecting men for a dacoitee", I replied, prove it if I have committed a theft or dacoitee. I'm ready to go to the jail if you can prove anything of that sort. The mahajons said, "If it costs us Rs. 100/-, we will see to that you are imprisioned." The Mahajons and the Daroga got very angry and the Daroga ordered the Mahajons and the police to tie me up, The Mahajons began to tie Sidu my brother......"

Amidst all these intolerable oppression, there was also a yearning deep down in the heart of every Santal for indepdence and for recognition as masters of the soil. This feeling in fact was the motivating force behind their struggle to establish a kingdom for themselves under their own tribal chiefs.

And in the winter of 1854 and 1855, the Santals began to be restless. They were determined to fight to regain freedom. They no longer wanted to be the serfs of the Hindus and slaves of the 'diku' mahajons. It was at this juncture the twin brothers, Sidu and Kanu hailing from the most oppressed village Bhognadi (half a mile from Barhait) stood-up to pilot the struggle. They claimed that they had received a mission from Thakurjiu to deliver their countrymen from the claws of their oppressors. They produced before the people the heavenly tokens as their credentials. The twinbrothers reported that they had been visited by Thakurjiu seven days in succession. At first in the form of a white man in Santal costume; next as a flame of fire, with a knife glowing in the midst; then as the perforated slice of a sal-trunk which forms the wheel of the Santals' bullock-cart. Their God delivered to them a sacred book and the sky showered down slips of blank-papers on which his people, the Santals were to write their own history. These papers were secretly spread throughout the Santal country. And each village recieved a scrap without a word of explanation. However, it had an implication as it would avoid the wrath of their national God, to forward it without a moment's pause to the nearest hamlet. Having in this way raised a general expectation of some great event among their country-men, the brothers expected the British Government to look into their grievances and re-dress them; but the Britishers had no time for them. They then appealed to the highest British authority in Calcutta for justice and they told them that their God has commanded them to wait no longer. They even warned the English commissioner saying if their grievances were not looked into, they themselves would re-dress them. As all their efforts failed, the desperate Santal leaders took the matter in their hand. They realized that their God was great and was too far; therefore, he works through his people; and that it was their turn to jump into action.

The Santals thus were driven to take-up the last resort they had. They despatched emissaries with their national sal-branch to every mountain valley. The people who had the fire of freedom firmly bruning in their hearts were obedient to the signal. They gathered in large numbers with bows and arrows in hand at Bhognadi on the 30th of June 1855 at full moon. The number of the people gathered is not known. However, the body-guards of the Santal leaders alone are said to be about 30,000 men. Their dormant character was stirred fury against their oppressors. The 'diku' mahajons and money-lenders indeed were ones of their targets; but the shrewed 'dikus' bribed the Britishers and turned the up-rising into a fight between the Santals and the British Government.

The resounding of Santal drum-beat fiilled the air, the Santal arrows flew like birds. The air was foul and bloody. The Santals dexterously fought the Britishers. But the native arrows were hardly a match for the British bullets. Over 10,000 Santals lost their lives in the battle. Finally, the British government managed to quell the fight in the year 1857.

As a result, the British government made some concession towards the Santals. The rebellion did bring about some significant changes in the relationship between the Santals and the politico-economic system of the British India. The establishment of a distinctive administrative territory within which the Santal interests were safe-guarded was the first measure taken by the Britishers. An area of 5,470 square miles was carved out of Bhagalpur and Birbhum districts and was explicity termed as 'Santal-Parganas'. Dumka, a place centrally located to the Santal population and somewhat isolated from the 'diku' interests was chosen for its administrative centre. The second measure was the importance given to the village headman. A large amount of the administrative power was vested on him.

And the third step taken was concerning land-rights. It became illegal for a Santal to transfer his ownership of land to any non-Santal.

The Santal 'Hul' that laid a foundation for freedom-fight of India has since been considered by historians a water shed' in Indian history.

A Christian mind links the Santal rebellion to the Biblical Exodus. The God of Exodus and the God of the Santals is the God on earth—a God who with his oppressed people is bent on breaking the 'rod' of the oppressors. It is the struggle of the Santals having their God as companian wanting to be free, want ing to be 'a people'. It is this struggle that becomes the starting point of our theologizing, a theologizing on the liberative action of God in the world on behalf of a 'non-people'. This in fact makes Christian theology a theology of liberation. Christian theology of liberation as James H. Cone would put, "is a rational study of the being of God in the world in the light of the existential situation of an oppressed community, relating to the forces of liberation to the essence of the gospel, which is Jesus Christ.'[3] We cannot speak of a Christian theology that does not identify itself with the people whose human dignity is deprived. The language of such a theology, therefore, is essentially a language of that is concerned with human liberation; proclaims the end of bondage, interprets the religious dimension of people's revolutionary struggle for freedom, and challenges social structures because of its inseparability from the suffering people of God. It is the contextual language that is defined by a concrete situation that gives birth to the Christian theology of liberation. No Christian theology can, therefore, be written for eternity and there can never be a theology for all ages, places and persons.

God's concern is not the abstract world, but his suffering people. The concern of Yahweh was his 'non-people', the Israel. The concern of Thakurjiu was his oppressed Santals. The consistent theme that runs through Israelite prophecy is Yahweh's concern for justice for those who are poor and unwanted in society. Yahweh in Hebrew prophecy does not tolerate injustice against the poor. The God of the Santals too does not tolerate the oppression done to his people. Theology, therefore, ceases to be a theology of the Bible, if it does not take root in the community of the oppressed.

In the New Testament, the theme of liberation is re-affirmed by Jesus himself (Lk. 4 : 18-19). The manifesto of Jesus is nothing else but the manifesto of the theology of liberation. Jesus manifested this freedom in his words and deeds. His death on the cross is the revelation of God's freedom, taking the totality of human oppression upon himself. And by raising Jesus from dead God discloses that he is not defeated by oppression, but reforms it into the possibility of freedom. For the Santals who continue to suffer oppression, this means that they do not have to behave as if death is the ultimate end of their suffering. It is this which gives them the eschatological hope of attaining "the milk of freedom" and "the honey of fellowship". The Santals will have to make their own history and write it down. The blank paper of Thakurjiu will have to bc filled in a proper manner.

CHAPTER 4

Human Person and Revelation

According to the traditional Christian understanding, the concept of 'Man'/'woman' consists of two elements, i.e., soul and body. The distinction between body and soul. in the words of O'Grady, "is based on an understanding of the body as the symbol of the soul and expressing the spiritual aspect of man".[4]

Revelation connotes "disclosure" or "divulgence". It is the act of making known what is abscure and hidden. This act, in the Judaeo-Christian tradition, exclusively belongs to God. God alone is the author and content of revelation. Revelation, therefore, is the divine self-disclosure.

Revelation is the communication of liberating knowledge. This implies that revelation is historical in the sense of historical liberation of an oppressed people from bondage. There cannot be an abstract revelation devoid of humnn experiences. God meets human person not as an idea or concept, but in her/his concrete life situation. He encounters her/him in her/his human condition as the liberator of the poor and the weak; and he empowers them to fight for freedom, for each woman/man is born to be free. Revelation in this sense can be liberation and the vice-versa. The scripture only speaks to our life situation, it does not make decisiions for us. The study of human person, therefore, is the illumination of revelation itself insofar as revelation occurs in the life of human person and nowhere else.

Human Person as the Creature of God (being in God's Image)

Human person, being the epitome of God's creation, was created in the image of God. The image of God in woman/man, one must keep in mind, is not photographic. In what way then is human person the image of God? Woman/man, according to Fichtner. "is made in the image of God insofar as he has : physical shape; a spiritual quality; the eternal turth; and good in him; reason; a divine spark; immortality; personality; self consciousness; dominion over the world; freedom; a relationship with God".[5] Human person has dominion over the rest of God's creation, and consequently. she/he is God's image. She/he must act on earth as God acted with regard to the universe and must manifest thc same qualities on earth that God manifested in creation. By doing so, woman/man shares in the glory of God. "The mercy and fidelity that are the characteristic virtue of God in the exercise of his dominion must also characterize the life and activities of man".[6]

Crertion is not only a past and mighty deed of God but also a present activity of God. Human person as created in the image of God does serve as the basis for all future development and working towards the fulfilment of creation. Woman/Man being in the image of God, therefore, implies divine call to represent God in creation, God chooses every woman/man to be his person for his greater glory. As St. Irenaeus remarked, 'The glory of God is man fully alive. There are two features of the divine image in woman/man from which accrues a basic human equality; viz every woman/man is created with a rational soul in God's image, because they take their nature and origin from him, and they are intrinsically alike. This in fact gives us an incentive to work for an egalitarian society.

Human person is Sinful : Every human person being sinful stands in need of redemption in Chirst: Woman 'man's sinfulness pre-supposes her/his freedom of choice. Freedom of choice can be said to be the capacity to act or not to act, to do this or to do that. It is by choosing to do things that are in consistent with the divine plan of creation, a person gets into the rut of sinfulness. Woman/Man lives in an evil world and contributes to that evilness by her/his own sin. One needs only to keep one's eyes open to realize this that human person is responsible to a very gaeat extent for the evil that is found in the world is an undeniable fact. Kiekegaard too places the responsibility of choice directly upon man.

St. Paul in his epistles speaks of two tendencies in woman/man as "inner-man" and "outer-man". He attributes the tendency to sin to outer-man and the tendency to virtue to the inner-man (2Cor. 4:16; Rom. 7:22; Eph. 3:16). There is a constant struggle between the inner-man and the outer man. The mere fact that these two tendencies are immanent in woman/man complements the sinful state of man/woman. And so, she/he stands in need of God's redemption in Christ.

"Those who are well have no need of a physician, but those who are sick......I came not to call the righteous, but sinners" (Mt. 9:12-13). On reading this passage, two obvious questions that puzzle our minds are:

> Would Jesus have come to this world if man/woman had never sinned ?
>
> Would woman/man needs God's saving help if he/she remains immaculate ?

Thesequestions can be dismissed in the words of Butter Worth :[7]

Even if man had never sinned, he would still have needed saving, in the sense that man was never originally meant to achieve, without God's further personal intervention, that fulfilment which man is eternally planned and created by God to attain.

And so, the more a Christian understands herself/himself the more she/he understands God and his son Jesus Christ. The more a believing community understands Jesus, the more it understands itself. If the Christian community is to appriciate the mystery of God in man, then, we must appriciate the mystery that is "MAN"·'/"WOMAN",

CHAPTER 5

A Kingdom-Centric Theology of Liberation

'The Kingdom of God'—'Malkut di elaha'— means "God rules". 'Basileia' or 'Malkut, is "reign" and not "realm" or "domain". It expresses (1) the activity of God establishing a new order—a revolution; and (2) Woman's/man's utopian longing for liberation from everything that alienates her/him. It is like the two sides of the same coin. The 'kingdom of God' does not evolve, rather it breaks in, turning the world up-side-down!

One can turn to the Book of Daniel to find the doctrine of 'the kingdom of God' in germ. There the message about 'the kingdom' is qualified as the good-news of pardon, peace, freedom from sin and death and friendship with God (Dan. 2 : 32 ff.). One may look up to Deutero-Isaiah and the Psalms for further enligntenment on ,the kingdom'.

The Notion of 'The Kingdom' in the Old-Testament :

The notion of the 'kingdom' does not stand for a place or dominion; rather it stands for 'action', the kingly activity of

God. In the Old-Testament we find two kingly actions of God, ie., creation and liberation. Through creation, God manifests himself as king (Ps. 47, 93, 96, 97—the enthronement songs). The Jews in fact saw the creation as salvation. The function of the king is basically to save his people. Therefore, 'El-Shaddai" 'the God of the hill' makes a covenant with his people (Ex. 6 : 2 ff.). It was a conveant of liberation form Egyptian slavery (Ex. 1 : 15), from starvation (Book of Numbers), from annihilation (Book of Joshua Judges; I and II Samuel), and from exile (Is. 40 :- 50). Indeed, the God of the Bible is a liberating God. He is the God who destroyes myths and alienation. The Biblical God is the one who intervenes in history in order to point out the way of justice and mercy. He is the God who liberates his pople from slavery. He causes empires to fall and raises up the oppressed.

Gutierrez, in his book "A Theology of Liberation", says, "The liberation of Israel is a poiitical action .... It is the suppression of disorder and the creation of a new order".[8] When we scrutinize the Exodus Event in the Bible, we find two critical elements that are fused into one, viz : God as the liberator, and the political process of liberation which leads His chosen race, the Israelites from the bondage in Egypt to the promised land, "a land flowing with milk and honey" (Ex. 3 : 8). This of course, is a symbol of prosperity and security (For a Jew, land is of theological value). They expected Yahweh to give them material prosperity in the promised land. Therefore, invariably their ideal future was bound-up with the land which Yahweh gave to their Fathers. It is to this kingdom the dregm of the kina Nebuchadnezzar in the Book of Daniel refers (Dan. 2 : 32 ff.). To the disappointment of the Jews, the people of Israel did not prosper like their neighbouring kingdoms. That led them to question God. Consequently, the fulfilment of the promise was projected to the future. Their attitude towards the promised land took a new dimension. "God will one day give us the land" was their hope. This gradually developed into messianic and apocalyptic hope : By messianic hope, the Jews believed, that God would oneday raise up a son of David who would establish a world empire where would be prosperity, i.e., land. Therefore they had the expectation of a Davidic messiah. By apocalyptic hope, they thought, oneday God would intervene in history once and for all to complete his work of liberation, his work of salvation. And so they hoped for an eschatological kingdom.

The Kingdom in the Synoptics :

The Bible is the record of the struggle of a non-people (poor), endeavouring to be people with God as their partner. The synoptic gospels express this in the term "the kingdom of God" (Mk. 1 : 14-16), designating God's reign or sovereign rule as king whereby he brings women/men the blessings of salvation. The messianic and apocalyptic hopes of the Old-Testament are summed up into this synoptic idea of the kingdom.

The kingdom of God in the synoptic gospel is the centre of Jesus' mission. It is for this that Jesus was chosen, anointed by the Spirit (Lk. 3 : 21-23) and tested (Lk. 4:1-13). All his words and deeds directly or indirectly were directed to the kingdom. Here, one must keep in mind that Jesus' teaching about the kingdom does not arise in a vacuum; but it is the fulfilment of something that was begun in the religious teaching of Israel.

In the synoptics, the mission of Jesus is the proclamation of the kingdom both in word and in deed. He expressed it in his person and in his works : He proclaims and works out salvation from sin (personal and structural), freedom from oppression, and proclamation of kingdom. "The kingdom of God is at hand; repent, and believe in the gospel" (Mk. 1 : 15) is the key text of the synoptics concerning Jesus' mission. The preaching of John the Baptist, the fore-runner of Jesus is related to the mission of Jesus. Jesus began to preach after John was arrested. Theologically, it was 'the sign of the time' for Jesus to preach and Jesus had waited for the right time (Mk. 1:15.). Fulfilment is much more than mere realization; It is the transcendental realization. Jesus can be called messiah only in the transcendental sense—namely, in relation to the Father's will. Liberation comes through the revelation of love; God's liberation therefore, consists in his revelation of love. Repentance means the turning of a person to God's love. According to Mark, repentance is to believe in the good-news that God loves you. Therefore, the kingdom of God is the revelation of God's love that not only calls for repentance, but also brings about freedom and leads to fellow-ship (doing good).

The "Abba experience" that precedes the proclamation is the basis and foundation of Jesus' mission (Mk. 1 : 9). In this, he experienced his Sonship with the Father (heaven torn opened), the feeling of brother-hood with his fellow-men (dove is the symbol of peace and brother-hood), and realized his life as a suffering servant. It is this experience of his solidarity with the "sinners" (those who were marginalized) that led him to social commitment. For Jesus, the social commitment was a religious experience. Love of neighbour is the medium of loving God (Mt. 25 : Mk. 12 : 28-34).

In this manifesto of the kingdom (Lk. 4 : 18-19), Jesus gives a social thrust. God's image is human person and human person is the concern of God; therefore, the sovereign rule of God essentially is in relation to man/woman whereby Jesus brings human beings the blessing of salvation. This sum total of proclamation is going to be the programme of Jesus' ministry. Healing and exorcism (over-throw of the kingdom of Satan, i.e., against an unjust system, sickness, possessions and dullness in order to integrate the afflicted into the society). Opposing religous oppressing (because of the Jewish religious ideology that is aroung the law and the temple), and denouncing social oppression (refering to the Gentiles, the Samaritans, the tax-collectors and sinners who were despised) were the praxis of the manifesto. "Misery and social injustice reveal' a sinful situation', a disintegration of brother-hood and communion; by freeing us from sin, Jesus attacks the root of an unjust order."[9]

The beatitudes relating to the kingdom is worth looking at. The sermon on the mount that follows the proclamation of the kingdom is the specific programme for those who follow Jesus. It is the consequence of the kingdom. Luke gives four "blessed" sayings and four "woe" sayings (Lk. 6 : 20-26). It is arranged in a reversal theme. A similar "blessed" passage is found in Mathew too (Mt. 5 : 3-11). Mathew gives an ethical slant to this passage while Luke gives it a sociological meaning. As the Ten Commandents are summed up in a double dimensional single commandments (i.e., loving God by loving our neighbours), so are the beatitudes summed up in a single beatitude in the gospel of Luke (6 : 20), "Blessed are you poor, for yours is the kingdom of God." Some scholars consider this to be the original and only beatitude of Jesus, and the rest to be later additions. Let us see what the words "poor", "Blessed", and "Yours" mean.

"Poor" can be interpreted sociologically, i.e., actually poor or made poor; dialectically, i.e., in relation to antagonists; and dynamically. i.e , they being the instrument of the kingdom. "Poor" in the gospel of Luke would mean those who are actually poor or made poor. (For the Bible undertands poverty as injustice). "Poor" in the gospel of Mathew is 'Anawim'—the person who puts his/her trust in God. However, they are intertwined. The oppressor obviously puts her/his trust in herself/himself not in God. Indeed it is the poor who possess an attitude of openness to God and spiritual child-hood. Poverty is "the ability to welcome God, a humility before God."[10]

"Blessed" because "Yours', is the kingdom of God. "Yours" because "the poor are the people who understand the meaning of the kingdom best, eventhough their knowledge and understanding comes by way of contraiety."[11] Jesus is the good-news for the poor because he brings them "justice" in its most comprehensive meaning: healing, forgiveness and wholeness.

Jesus' saying "The kingdom of God is in the midst of you" (Lk. 7 : 21) indicates that 'the kingdom of God' specifically refers to him. And Jesus in his person and in his works and words represented it (Words and actions go hand-in-hand according to the gospel tradition). "But if I cast out devils by the Spirit of God then the kingdom of God has come upon you" (Mt. 12 : 38). Therefore, the kingdom of God is not something that we have to wait for somewhere in the future.

The kingdom of God for Jesus places a radical demand on man/woman. "No one who puts his hand to plough and looks back is fit for the kingdom of God" (Lk. 9 : 62). That is because Jesus considers the kingdom as the absolute value; and everything else is relative. "Leave the dead to burry their dead; but you, go and proclaim the kingdom of God" (Lk. 9 : 60).

The kingdom of God is not static. Jesus gave a goal-directing norm and not a blue-print of the kingdom. He considered the kingdom to be dynamic and growing. The kingdom of God has come, and yet to come; therefore, Jesus asks his disciples to pray. (The eschatological kingdom of course, is the kingdom of the beatitudes).

Jesu s as the prophet of the kingdom :

The prophet is "a man who feels fiercely. God has thrust a burdon upon his soul, and he bowed and stunned at man's fierce greed. Frightful is the agony of man; no human voice can convey its full terror"[12] He is the one who confronts his contemporaries with the will of God as revealed in history by way of announcing, denouncing and calling.

Prophetism was a specific, peculiar, primary and constitutive element of Judaism. In fact, the very being and mission of Israel was constitutive of prophetism (Deut. 18 : 17ff.). It is the prophetic orientation of Jesus that links Jesus with the Biblical world. Jesus being more in the line of Moses supplements the prophetism of Judaism. However, we cannot rule out the difference between them. The difference between Moses and Christ is that the law came through Moses while grace and truth came through Jesus.

The call of the twelve men by Jesus (the number of the tribes of Israel) was an acted parable in the manner of the old Testament prophets. "By his choice of twelve men Jesus proclaimed his intention to create a new Israel; and wherever he appeared with his twelve men, the number itself would say to all men of insight, 'This is the messiah and the new people of God."[13]

Jusus' proclamation of the kingdom in Galilee shows it clear; his consciousness of being in the prophetic line as a contiuner of the prophetic hope of a divine kingdom. There is an opinion among some exegetes that Jesus might have joined he Baptist who streesed universality and morality in his mission.

As the prophet of the kingdom Jesus denounced socio-economic and religous oppression. He also responded to the policies and practices of the political leaders of his time and by doing that he overthrew the kingdom on Satan. He announced the present natre of the kigdom. While representing the kingdom in his very person and in his works, he also summoned people for action, for repentance. Jesus was a prophet of the kingdom by his word and action. The entry into Jerusalem, the cursing the fig-tree, and the demonstration in the temple (Mk. 11 : 11ff.) were some of his conspicuous prophetic symbolic actions. As any other prophet, suffering was forced on him too. And ultimately, the death on the cross was the penalty he had to pay for being the prophet of the kingdom.

Human kind redeemed in and through Christ :

Man/Woman is ever becoming. His/her becoming is made possible by the fact that he/she is open to transcendence. Human person's becoming and his/her transcendence form he basis for all of the creativity of life. God as the transcendent cause gives to his creation the power to become. He supports and sustains his creation in its ever developing journey to perfection. In this process, he sent his son Jesus to the world. Christ, 'the word made flesh' for us Christians is truly the revelation of God. He was the man par excellence in whom every man finds his supreme realization. His mission, and ours in turn, is to free mankind from everything threatening to its full humanity.

St. Paul alludes in his epistle to the Colosians (Col. 3 : 9-10) to the Book of Genesis (Gen. 1 : 26) while dealing with the idea that man/woman is renewed in the image of the creator, the Christ. He also speaks of man being "clothed" wiih this in the sacrament of baptism (Gal. 3 : 27). Baptism for him is an endowment of connatural knowledge which transforms man into the real, genuine image of God. According to him, the old man was fallen human nature; the new man was a new creation that was affected by baptism (Rom. 6 : 6; Eph. 4 : 22; Col. 3 : 9).

To grow fully into Christ is to partake in his Sonship that makes us similar, really and truly, like a blood brother, to the first-born of all men (Rom. 8 : 29-30; 2 Cor. 3 : 17-18). This similarity to Christ is realizable "not by some ethical imitation of Christ, simply because he was a 'good man', but through his grace."[14]

The Kingdom in Santal context

Kingdom is the name for liberation; and our God is a God who liberates. What does liberation mean in today's world? Liberation, according to Gutierrez:[15]

(i) Expresses the aspirations of the oppressed people and social classes, emphasizing the conflictual aspect of the economic, social and politieal process which puts them at odds with wealthy nations and oppressive classes;

(ii) Can be applied to an understanding of history. Man seen as assuming conscious responsibility for his own destiny. This understanding provides a dynamic context and broadens the horizons of the desired social changes. In this perspective the unfolding of all of man's dimensions is demanded—a man who makes himself through his life and throughout history. The gradual conquest of true freedom leads to the creation of a new man and a qualitively different society. This vision provides, therefore' a better understanding of what infac is t at stake in our times; and

(iii) In the Bible, Christ is presented as the one who brings us liberation. Christ the saviour liberates man from sin, which is the ultimate root of disruption of friendship and of all injustice and oppression. Christ makes man truly free, that is to say, he enables man to live in communion with him; and this is the basis for all human brother-hood.

Against the above back-drop, let us have a photo-glance view of the Indian situation :

The mode of production essentially depends on the relation of production to consumption and the vise-versa. On this stands the Indian economic structure. There is a super-structure comprising of a political structure to defend the status quo and an ideological structure consisting of philosophy, law and religion to justify the same. The socio-political situation is gravely unjust, unequal that is pervasive and cumulative.

(1) ECONOMIC DISCREPANCY

(a) *Unequal sharing of nation's wealth* :

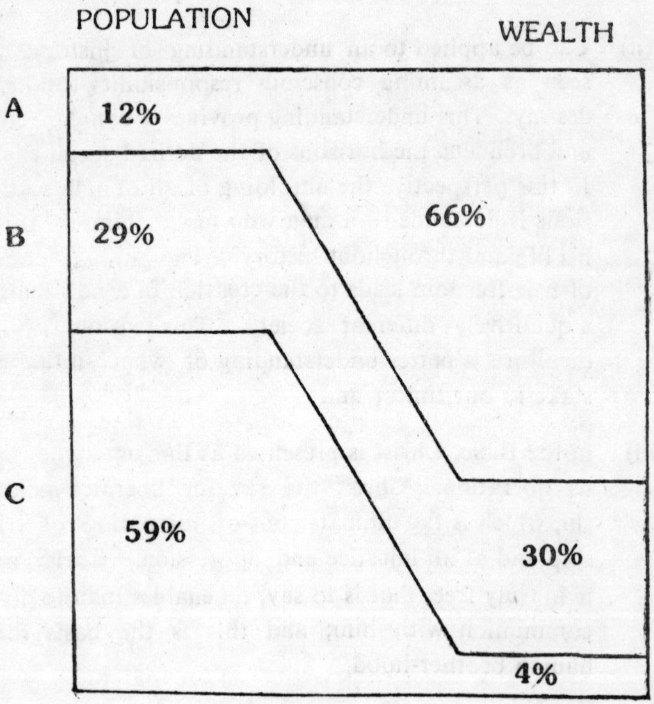

12%—1.2% very rich. They include top industrialists, Film Stars, black marketeers.

12%—Just below are the affluent class or capitalist class. They include top bureaucrats, top professionals, vast majority of the leaders of the country, jamindars, industrialists, money-lenders etc.

(Sociologists place the Church in the top 10% of this class).

29%—Middle Class.

59%—Poor Class.

(b) *Land Concentration in rural areas* :

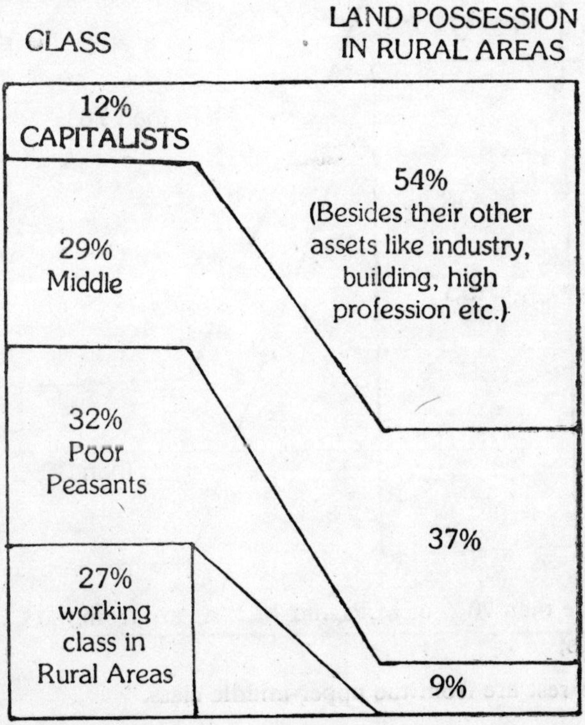

12%—Capitalist class possess 54% of land in the rural areas besides their other assets like industry, buildings, high profession etc.

29%—Middle class possess only 37% land.

32%—Poor peasants possess only 9% land.

27%—Working class in the rural areas have no land at all.

(2) POLITICS

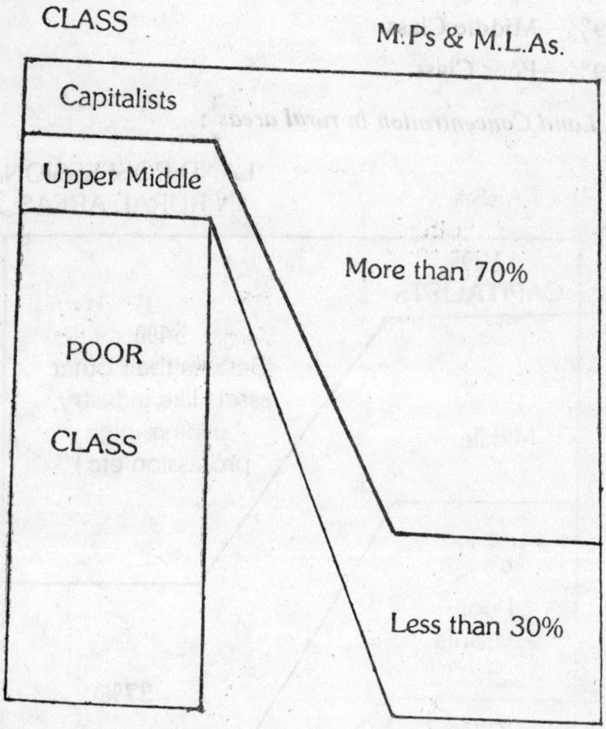

More than 70% of M.Ps and M.L.As are from the Capitalist class;

The rest are from the upper-middle class.

There's harly any from the poor class.

Therefore, the government is in the hands of the rich.

(3) BASIC NEEDS

(a) *Food* :

While the rich class feast with very expensive and imported food and drink, the poor cannot get even coarse grain. While the food storages are bulging, the stomach of the poor are empty and dry.

(b) *Clothing* :

While stores and cupboards of the rich are filled with fashionable and expensive clothes, there is no cheap cloth available for the poor class. The per capita availability of cotton cloth has declined between 1958-65 and 1980-85, by about 7.6%.

(c) *Shelter* :

Rich class possess very rich mansions with the latest facilities and comforts.

60% of the poor class have only thatched huts.

25 million people have no roof over their heads.

In cities 33% of the population are pavement dwellers.

(4) HEALH

In India every minute 3 children die of diarrhoea (i.e., 1.5 million per year).

40,000 children go blind because of vitamine deficiency.

84% of sickness is due to poor drinking water facilities.

Health care facilities :

	Urban	*Rural*
Doctors	70-80%	20-30%
Nurses	60%	40%
Hospitals	74%	26%
Dispensories	20%	70%

"There is a police behind ev'ry 250 Indians while there is only one doctor for 3500 people."

—V.P. Singh.

(5) EDUCATION

The World Bank estimates, India would have the largest concentration of illiterate population in the world by the year 2000 A.D.;

The country will have 54.8% of world's illiterate population in the age group 15-19.

(6) WOMEN

* Victims of exploitation and injustice
* No voice in society
* Religiously she's under bondage
* No right to property
* Victims of meanigless customs and practices
* Marriage has become a business transaction
* Bride burning and feminine infanticide.

(7) SERVICE

74% of the rural population render service to 25% of the urban population.

25% of the urban population offer their service to 17% of the rural population.

(8) CASTE : (class+caste=claste)

There are over 2,000 castes in India, but most of them are limited geographically.

Accoring to 1971 census, about 6% population is Brahmines while 14.7% population is Dalits (Harijans). In some states however, the proportion of Dalit is higher (eg.) Tamil Nadu has over 18% dalits. Today, their number all over the country has crossed well over 100 miliion.

Dalits (Harjians) are considerd the dregs, the untouchables of the society. Untouchability does not surface when it comes to sexual exploitation !

(9) RELIGION

As in socio-economic and political sphere, it is the elite minority that determines the type of God to be worshipped by the majority. It is they who prescribe the type of worship. And such cultic religion invariably projects the image of pomp loving, greedy and gluttonous God.

Thus the top minority having all economic, political knowledge and power, do guide the destiny of the large majority. The vast marginalized masses infact live at the mercy of the minority.

It is a fast developing capitialistic and managerial type of situation. Besides, there is also a mounting up of cultural crisis as a consequence of the tension between the traditional values and modernity, and integral humanism and capitalism. Side-by-side we also see a constant struggle for liberation in the Indian society. Numerous liberation movements keep springing up all over India, People are evermore becoming class conscious. And there is a deep sense of anger and disappointment in the masses.

Compounded by such exploitative societal structure exist the Santal social structures. The aggressive pyramidal Indian social structure today more than ever is cancerously affecting the circular tribal structure of the Santals driving them to non-existence. As I have elaborately discussed, the crisis the Santal society is facing today from its various angles in the first chapter of this book, I do not intend to repeat them here. However, the hard fact is that the Santal society today is in a very critical situation; it is on its way to being "faced-out". Tribal life is speedily becoming a non-entity in India. "Indeed, I tremble for my country when I reflect that God is just", says Thomas Jefferson.

What does liberation, the kingdom of God, mean in this context for Santal Parganas? For a Christian, the oppression of man/woman undeniably is a humiliation of God. Bringing about the kingdom in the given situation of Santal Parganas is necessarily bound-up with fighting against injustice. Justice is as much a necessity for Santal Parganas as breathing is; therefore, this should be the constant occupation of the Santals today. "The struggle for justic", rightly assents Dom Antonio Fragaso, "is also the struggle for the kingdom of God". The gospel of Christ today, therefore. implies man's/women's multiple efforts to obtain justice.

CHAPTER 6

Liberation and the Church

Christianity is essentially a religion of liberation. The Church, then is the community of the faithful living on the basis of the radical demands of the gospel and thus making the gospel a secular reality. This would necessarily mean that any message that is not closely linked to the liberation of the 'poor' and the 'weak' in a society, particularly in the Santal society is not Christ's message. To preach the gospel in Santal-Parganas today would mean confronting the oppressive forces with the reality of Christian freedom. Only by doing so can the Santal Church participate in Jesus' liberating work in history.

The fundomental option of the Church : The Galilean ministry of Jesus was his actual working out of the decision that was expressed in his birth and was re-affirmed by his 'Abba experience'. The tempter's obvious concern was to divert Jesus from the hard reality of his mission with the poor and the oppressed. Jesus' refusal to the tempter may be interpreted as his non-compliance with the prevailing oppressive mode of life or the self-glorifying power.

"No one can be a man who has not discovered something for which he is prepared to die"[16]. The condemnation of Jesus to death on the cross indicated that the Jews clearly saw the option he was posing to them. Their choice was between the God of their religion and the God of Jesus. They had to choose between the God of their religion and the God of Jesus. They had to choose between the temple and human beings; between the security provided by their own good works and the insecurity of God's gratuitous coming in grace. Man/woman can choose, but can't choose well—that was the case with the Jews. Consequently suffering and the death on the cross was forced on Jesus as a penalty for being the prophet of the kingdom taking a stand with the poor and the oppressed of his time. In historical terms God is to be found in the crosses of the poor and the oppressed Santals rather than in beauty, power or wisdom.

The same option the Jews of Jesus' time had before them is the option for us today—may be in different forms. Can the institutional Santal Church that is intrinsically woven into the feudal, capitalistic and semi-colonial Indian society be a Church of the poor and oppressed Santals? The organized and structured Church in the Santal land can be placed within the top 10% of the Indian social pyramid. This obviously puts it in a rather uncomfortable position to preach the Gospel : "Blessed are the poor". (Mt. 5 : 3). To be a liberating Church in Santal-Parganas today is not an easy task. It implies the authentic contexualization of the church in the historical situation of the Santals. It means breaking with all the oppressive forces and with those whose interest is to maintain the status quo. The bare fact is that the Santal church for long has been turning a blind eye to the oppressed Santals. The call of Christ today, therefore, is one of commitment to the poor and weak Santals—a call to be a Church of Christ.

Church in Santal Home-Land : The Church can be defined as the totality of the faithful of God in their concrete societal and cultural situations. To be the Church of the people, it has to take root and flourish in the soil of its people. Jesus by his very life clearly showed us that ' the first duty of the redeemer is to incarnate himself among those whom one seeks to redeem and to flesh-out a life at their level, paying heed to the dynamics of the real historical situation"[17]. Attempts have been made since years at inculturation—Vatican-II gave some impetus to it yet it has borne meagre fruit. One wonders as to why the Church, particularly the Santal Church, is not very successful in this sphere.

To inculturate herself, the Church must have a theology that effect, because theology "mediates between a cultural matrix and the significance and role of religion in that matrix".[18] Therefore, the comprehensive picture of the people of Santal-Parganas in their respective socio-cultural context has to be drawn clearly before the eyes, prior to opening the Bible to find God's message for them.

The authentic contextualization of the Church in the Santal home-land is her prophetic mode of living in the given historico-cultural situation. That is, the church has to live a life that witnesses Christ who emptied himself and became one among the poor and the oppressed and fought against the oppression to the extent of laying down his very life. This implies that the Church will have to give up her structual status, emptying herself to identify with the poor and the oppressed, to stand against whatsoever form of oppression and to strive to set-up an egalitarian society.

A growing awareness of the massive social evil that plague the Santal land today must serve as the basis of our theology. A

Santal theologian who is exposed to social analysis must feel challenged by the existing oppressive situation of the Santals.

Theology, therefore, must allow itself to be converted by the poor and the oppressed Santals to be free to serve the people in discovering the full liberative meaning of the gospel in their situation.

The service demanded of the Santal theology in Santal situation today is one of establishing an egalitarian society in which every Santal man and woman live as brothers and sisters belonging to one family of God.

'A Santal Theology of Libeation' that aims at the localization of the Church must also call for the re-working of the sacramental life of the Church to that effect. It must insist on the Church's celebration of her faith in signs and symbols taken from the life and culture of her people, ensuring a tone of liberation.

The sacramental rites and rituals have come under fire in Santal home-land especially in the last two decades. This is mostly in relation to the problem of 'nominal' or 'sunday' Christians. Two very prominant reasons that could be attributed to it are :

(i) Lack of understanding of the meaning and implications of the sacraments; and

(ii) The sacramental rites do not touch upon the Santal cultural sacramentality.

These two, as we see, are inter-related. To understand the meaning and implications of the Sacramental rites necessitates total inculturation. The Santal Church for long has over-emphasized uniformity of rituals and turned blind eye to the cultural sentiments of the Santals. It's concern should be unity and not uniformity, for uniformity curtails human freedom. A

Church that strives to set man/woman at liberty must necessarily negate unformity and foster unity. The Romen sacramental rites of the Santal Church by and large have remained' a potted-plant' without really being trans-planted. And so, it remains alien to the Santal ethos and un-understood by them. Therefore, it is the task of Santal theologians to re-think and re-formulate the rites and rituals of the Santal Church taking into account of the Cultural sentimentalities of the Santals. A culturally integrated sacramental rite first and fore-most safeguards the cultural identity and security of the Santals; that is to say, the people are not isolated from their non-Christian tribal milieu. Secondly, it inculcates a feeling of sentimental attachment to the sacraments.

The Roman liturgical texts that are used in mass and the sacramental celebrations in general do not help the Santals very much to grasp what dying and rising with Jesus really means. The liturgical celebration must feature its liberative aspect. It must make the participants march towards their liberation. A liturgy devoid of this liberative over-tone may end up in being a 'opium' for the poor and the oppressed. The Eucharistic celebration is an endorsement of "the act of the Father who radically negated the injustice by which the sin of the world victimized the just one"[19]. This reminds me of the protest mass celebrated in Columbia. This, then, is a brief outline of how a liberation liturgy would look like: "It would have penitential, prophetic, and sacrificial features, culminating with the people's shared communion of the fruits of this sacrifice."[20]

As an effort to inculturate herself, the Santal Church must pay ample attention to her art and architecture. The Christian art and architecture must reflect Santal Cultural patterns. One often wonders whether the buidings put up by the institutional Santal Church in Santal home-land are the felt need of the Santal faithful. Through the necessity of putting up church buildings (absolutely) cannot be ruled-out, a carefully thought-out buildings would minimize cultural alienation. Another discrepency that prevents the Santal Church from being entirely ecclesiogenesis is its financial dependency on the west. A self-supporting church, as we know, is the ideal. Achieving this ideal is the challenge faced by the Santal Church today. There are signs; a significant number of priests and religious are already marching towards it. For the church to be ecclesio-genesis, promotion of local Santal vocations is a must. Little has been done in this regard by the Santal Church.

SANTAL & NON-SANTAL PRIESTS AND NUNS IN DUMKA DIOCESE

Bishop	1
Diocesans	28
Jesuits	39
Salesians	6
TORs	2
Total	76

Number of non-Santal priests	—	71
Number of Santal priests	—	5
Total number of Sisters	—	103
Number of non-Santal Sisters	—	91
Number of Santal Sisters	—	12

Source : Status Animarum, 1989.

TOTAL POPULATION & CATHOLICS IN INDIA

Total population	Catholics	% of total population
683,810,000	11,707,000	1.71%

Diocesan Priests in India

1981 — 7058

Religious

Priests (1981)	—	4943
Men other than priests	—	2801
Women	—	49956

Total Population	—	800 million
Dalits	—	105 million
Tribals	—	60 million

Source : Catholic Directory of India, 1984.

CATHOLIC SANTAL SCENE

Catholic missionary work among the Santals started in 1862.

There are 19 dioceses where Santals are found.

The dioceses of Nepal, Bangladesh, Dumka, Bhagalpur and Raiganj have put aside some personnel to work among the Santals :

There are about 600 Santal Catholics in Nepal
22,000 in Bangladesh

65,000 Dumka
50,000 Bhagalpur — Santal core dioceses
20,000 Raiganj

CHRISTIAN SANTAL

Out of 8 million Santals there are 3 lakhs of Christians

2 laks Catholics and 1 lakh Protestants.

NELC	:	50,000
CNI	:	25,000
Baptist Union	:	10,000 (Bangladesh & W. Dinajpur)
American Baptist	:	10,000 (Midnapur, Balasore, Singbhum Districts)
Episcopal Methodist	:	3,000 (Pakur, Asansol)
Adventists	:	1,000 (Karmataur)
Pentacostals	:	300 (Nepal) and more.

SANTAL RELIGIOUS PERSONNEL

32 dioceasan Priests

10 religious Priests

30 Major Seminarians & Scholastics in formation

40 Brothers (32 M.C. Brothers)

150 Sisters (30 M.Cs, 30 C.T.Cs, 25 D.S.A. and Bambinas; 21 Santi Ranis, 15, HoCs; 5 Sisters of Mary Help of Christians etc.).

A BRIEF SURVEY OF DUMKA CATHOLIC DIOCESE

Part—I

A. 1. Diocese DUMKA

2. Boundaries/Area

Bihar :	Purnea Dt.	
	Katihar Dt.	Area : 22,814 sq. kms.
	Sahibganj Dt.	(details of this are
	Dumka Dt.	available)
	Part of Deoghar Dt.	
W. Bengal :	Rampurhat Sub-div. of Birbhum Dt.	

3. Population

(according to 1981 Census)

Purnea Dt.	3,585,707
Katihar Dt.	1,428,622
S.P. Dt.	2,759,401
Rampurhat S—D	865,271
	8,649,001

Catholics : (according to PPs reports)	Local :	52,625
	Foreigners	35
		53,660

From Census 1981 :

	X' tians	*Hindus*	*Muslims*	*Other Religions*	*Other Persuasions*	*RNS**	*Total*
(Bihar)	740,186	58,011,070	9,874,993	108,320	1,179,878	287	69,914,734
Katihar	2,437	994,917	550,596	2,476	182	22	1,550,627
Purnea	3,702	2,175,203	1,518,473	8,026	146	32	3,705,582
S.P.	61,049	2,923,412	611,367	2,169	119,431	100	3,717,528

*RNS=Religion Not Stated.

Details of Other persuasions :

Other Persuasion	*India*	*Bihar*	*Katihar*	*Purnea*	*Santal Parganas*
1	2	3	4	5	6
Adivasi	25,416	15,862		45	7,079
Arab	353	92			22
Atheist	24,086	891		30	27
Bengali	2,982	34			4
Bidin	1,296	1,296			1,246
Bonga	327	327			327
Gujarati	2,487	1			1
Kharwar	12,168	12,134			745
Manab Dharma	816	90			2
Munda	1,160	674		8	
Nepali	1,615	77		7	

(*Contd.*)

1	2	3	4	5	6
Paharia	1,813	1,746			1,746
Santals (in 5 States)	32,252	20,814	172	9	17,336
Swarna	1,391,178	1,101,436	5		89,813
Protestants		1,155,174	179	145	118,370
Anand Marg				3	3
Arya Samaj					50
Harijan					7
Kabir Panthi			2	3	
Sanatan Dharma			551	811	469
Satsangi					4
Sindhu					3
Vaishav			18	18	2
Vedic Dharma			5	2	32

4. Language spoken : Hindi, Urdu, Santali......

Literacy rate

	Percentage		
	Female	*Male*	*Total*
Purnea	9.39%	24.41%	19.27%
Katihar	11.34%	30.03%	21.03%
(old S.P. Dt.)	10.52%	34.49%	22.26%
Dumka Dt.	6.36%	25.85%	16.57%
Godda Dt.	5.24%	24.92%	15.35%
Sahibganj Dt.	6.99%	20.69%	13.97%
Deoghar Dt.	7.90%	30.80%	19.87%
(State)	13.62%	38.11%	26.20%

B. 1. Number of parishes in Diocese 18

Number of secular priests 23

2. Number of religious priests 49
3. Number of religious brothers 17
4. Number of religious Sisters 191
5. Any other ... ... (Secular Inst.) 3

C. Number of Teacher

		Religious		*Laity*	
	No.	*M.*	*F.*	*M.*	*F.*
Primary Schools	82	25	28	131	133
Middle Schools High Schools	19	21	6	40	26
Religious Insti.	2				

D. Social Welfare Centre

1. Home for Poor Children : Kundli/Dudhani/Katihar (MCs)? Mixed
2. Home for Aged : Dudhani/Kundli (MCs)
3. Home for Handicapped
4. No. of non-subsidized Hostels/Boardings : 2 (SX+CS)

   No. of subsidized hostels/boardings : 29

   for boys : 16—Inmates 2,599

   for girls 13—Inmates 1,879
5. Creches : Dudhani/Kundli (is this the same as no. 1 above).
6. Hospitals : 2 (Cil.+Pur) No. of beds in each : 20
7. Health Centres : 18
8. Vocational Training Centres : all Grihinis (MP, Jiapani, Jamtara)
9. Work Centres : Dudhani

E. Others

1. Printing Presses : 1

   Publications : 1
2. Associations : Katholik Sabha

   Mahila Sangh

   Krus Vir

   Maria Marg.

Church and politics : 'Politics' is the 'rule of polis', i.e., the 'science of government'. It connotes a total complex of relationships among human beings in society. Politics comprises of two major element; viz; a vision and an option. While the vision sets the goal to be achieved in a society or for a society, the option serves as a means to achieve that goal. Both imply choice; and the choice can be for the betterment of a concerned society or it may also be of one that leads a community to doom. In this sense, we can speak of human reason becoming a political reason, for one's reasoning is essentially seen against the back-drop of the historical situation in which one is. Every theology, therefore, "is political even one that does not speak or think in political terms"[21].

Though politics comprises of every aspect of human life in a society, it could also be taken as a structure that constitutes the organizational structure of a society. However, it cannot be thought of as a water-tight compartment. Jesus, therefore, responded not only to the social situation of the poor and the weak, but also to the political policies and practices of the leaders of his time. His emphatic denunciation of the socio-religious practices could not but interfere with the entire socio-political power structure. "Take up your cross" in the time of Jesus had a clear political tone, for it was with the cross the political rebels of his time were punished by the state. Crucifixion was a typical Roman punishment for the Zealot rebels. Jesus claimed himself to be the Messiah, the king. He had the sons of Thunder (James and John) and Simon 'barjona' (meaning terrorist) as his diciples. This implies a definite political import in Jesus' messianic mission. And for this he was put to death a political criminal.

Church is a sign of union with God and unity with the people who live in a concrete historical situation. It is a prophetic community that keeps challenging its comtemporaries. "As a prophetic community, and an eschatological sign, the church is essentially political......because the objectified character of the public community is nothing else but the social and political body of human beings united together"[22]. And so, the church must jump in and join the struggle for justice taking a form of political struggle for life through death, even death on the cross. In its struggle for justice, the church must necessarily live a sacramental life that evokes a response in each Christian to that effect. Unfortunately our present Christian worship seems to smack of triumphalism, cultural alienation and irrelevance. An apolitical liturgy in a world that is essentially political is absurd. An apolitical liturgy either separates the people from their concern with the world or it makes them fatalistic. This is what Karl Marx terms as religion being the 'opium' of the people. Quite often the church in her history deafened her ears to the voice of Christ and listened to the voice of the ruling class and their selfish interests. All these are against the basic principle of the being a liberation movement of its faithful. "A political option in favour of liberative change is an intrinsic element of faith and helps to de-idealogize the latter. We can only have an authentic faith, in other words, when we have committed ourselves to an authentic struggle that opens our eyes to the new possiblities and meaning of God's word"[23]. This is precisely the Christian vocation tending towards activities that are political.

Church's Mission Today: The Church is a movement of believers in Christ and his values for realizing his vision of a new society—the Kingdom. The Chruch is neither final nor universal, but only a witness to him who is risen and has achieved fullness. As vanguard and sign, the Church is an imperfect and obscure image; however, it is true enough to be recognizable in the power of the Spirit. Though it has already been inaugurated, it still awaits its complete form, viz, the unique, ultimate and universal reign of God. In her entire existence, in all that she is and does during the period between the Easter and Parousia, the Church is there to make her prophetic proclamation and be an image and representation of that which is promised to all.

The conciliar Church, therefore, sees itself as a missionary Church (Cf. LG- no: 16ff; AG. no: 35ff). Its dogmas and its interpretations of scripture are not an end in themselves; their purpose is to serve the world-wide mission of the Church. This means that the Church must do more than preserve the purity of its doctrine intra mures. In bearing witness to the faith, it must render service to human society and try to answer the questions of mankind (Cf. GS. 40, 58, 76, 87). The communion with the Lord inescapably means a Christian life centred around a concrete and creative commitment of service to others.

Faith and justice are mutually constitutive. Action for justice and transformation of the world stands out for us as the essential reason for preaching the Gospel. This in fact is the mission of the Church concerning the redemption and liberation of mankind from every oppression. It is "by preaching the Gospel message, by its sacraments and by charity of its members", says Gutierrez, "that the Church proclaims and shelters the gift of the kingdom of God in the heart of human history. The Christian community professes a 'faith which works through charity'. It is...atleast ought to be...real charity, action and commitment to the service of man"[24].

Each new situation in the world, each understanding of man and society, brings a new challenge to the church. However, the Church for centuries devoted her attention to formulating truths and meanwhile did almost nothing to better the world. The Santal church too on her part has failed to come to grip in praxis with the structual problems. However, there is certain awakenting in the Santal Church particularly that of Dumka today. Some priests and religious want the church to break her ties with an unjust order. They want her to cast her lot with the Santals who suffer from misery and deprivation.

The Santal Church's foremost concern today should be neither Christ nor the Bible, but the Santals, the people of God in Christ. The attitude of the Church in fact is based on the understanding that the coming of the kingdom implies the building up of a just society. This of course, calls for a conversion of heart. Conversion is indeed the touch-stone of all spirituality. It means a radical transformation of oneself. It means thinking, feeling and living as Jesus who is present in the exploited and alienated Santals. To be converted is to commit oneself to the process of liberation of the poor and oppressed Santals, to commit oneself lucidly realistically and concretely. And it is only by doing so will the Church be a witness in Santal-Parganas, to the new creation that was inaugurated by Christ.

CHAPTER 7

Action and Violence

To be true to our Christian life demands commitment to the liberation of the poor and the oppressed; and that implies our involvement in the secular and political struggles of the Santals. Any involvement in view of liberation necessarily implies a break with the status quo and calls for a radical revolution which is the gift Christ offers us. Camilo Torres is right in saying that a revolutionary action for liberation is 'a Christian' and 'a priestly' struggle. To place oneself in the perspective of the kingdom in Santal-Parganas means to participate in the ongoing struggle for liberation of the oppressed Santals. "If the Church identifies itself with the struggle of the oppressed, it will run head-on into the oppressors who hold power. But only in this way can the Church serve as an irrefutable sign of the fact that it is dedicated to the establishment of justice no matter what the cost".[25] However, one must not forget that the liberation of the poor and the liberation of the rich are achieved simultaneously. Genuine struggle for liberation always must emerge from below. To be authentic, it must be undertaken by the oppressed Santals themselves; for they who are in need of liberation must choose to be liberated. It must stem from their freedom of choice. Yet, for the success on any revolutionary activity, it has to be manoeuvred by a middle-class intellectual groups.

Kingdom of God is the object of violence (Cf. Mt. 11 : 12 : Lk. 16:16). In the unjust society today, militancy of faith is a must. We can speak of two forms of violence, the violence of the unjust oppressor which is original and aggressive and the violence that is performed on behalf of the oppressed, the violence with which God punishes the unjust oppressors irrespective of their being an individual or a group or even a nation. Therefore, violence in the strict sense would mean "the injustice which deprives man of his personal rights by force and prevents him from giving shape to his personal life on this basis of his own personal judgement."[26]

A God without wrath, James Cone would say, does not intent to do too much of liberating. But we know from the Bible that the God of Israelites was warrier God (Ex. 15: 1b-3). (Whoever sheds the blood of man, by man shall his blood be shed") (Gen. 9 : 6) was the stand the God of Genesis took. A fine sense of justice like 'an eye for an eye and tooth for a tooth' was up-held by all the peophets and psalmist. The nation is still called upon to fight against oppression to which it is subjected (Ps. 137). The Psalmist does not regard the punishment of an unjust person in power as something violent. The sinfulness depends therefore on whether it is perpetrated in the just or unjust cause. The prophets fermented violence when it was for the good of the masses; other-wise, they forbade it. The God of Israelites is the same unchanging God even today. To portray the love of God as unconditional in an oppressive society is be-littling God himself. Jesus in his earthly ministry was violent and he encountered violence. His death and resurrection was the consummation of that. "Only idealistic over-simplification of Jesus' real attitudes" in the words of

Segundo, "can paint a picture of him as a human being dedicated to limitless love without a trace of resistence or violence". That Jesus was driven to the point of picking-up a whip in hand and driving away the merchants from the temple of Jerusalem is of minor importance. That the attack on the very roots of the phoenician woman's national identity in-order to test her was of no importance.

Can militancy of faith become violent in Santal-Parganas today? To say that, one must weigh the cost not only of violence, but also of Gandhian 'ahimsa' in a country liks ours. A Santal liberation today is a revolution...'a turning the world up-side-down'. It is a collective action of the poor and the weak Santals to free them-selves from every kind of bondage and oppression...economic, social, political, cultural and religious. It is through this revolutionary activity, can the Santals realize heir own humanity by taking control of history and becoming makers of their own destiny. At the heart of this committed action lies a certain conception of human life, a sense of worh and dignity of every Santal person. This is the challenge every Santal is faced with, which none of of them can evade.

CHAPTER 8

Theologizing in Santal-Parganas

Theology is a critical and committed reflection on the historical faith experience which leads to action-rellection-action that transforms life. But whose faith experience?...the experience of the theologian OR Is it the experience of the community ? What is the relation between the theologian and the community ? Culture provides the context of reflection as well as becomes a tool for it. Which culture ? Is it an imported sub-culture OR Is it the culture that is proper to the people of the locality?

We encounter God not in vacuum, but as men and women inserted at a particular point in the flux of Santal history. And so, we are and must be conditioned by the Santal social system and culture. What the Santals need in Christianity is not a growth by means of assimilating a culture that is alien to their own, but incarnation. The Santals have suffered enough from the colonizing theology. An imported western 'diku' theology is not theology for them. They must have their own theology—a theology that liberates them from every form of oppression, a theology that is specific of their own. If there can be a theology for the Black, if there can be a western theology, and

Indian theology, a Tribal theology, there can also be a theology for the Santals—a "Hoṛ Theology". If the 'diku' theology can have its own terminology, the Santals can also have their own terminology. They no more want a 'diku' theology to dictate terms for them. They are capable of dictating terms to themselves. Theirs is the 'Rat in Cat's mouth' theology—a theology of the oppressed people not the other way about.

Theologizing in Santal Parganas, therefore, should be a critical, committed reflection on Santal history in and through which comes the self manifestation of the divine targetting at a renewed engagement to establish God's kingdom. The western theology by and large is (mis) understood only as an interpretation of sacred texts. Theology is much mose than that. It must essentially be an interpretation of human reality. The prime concern of any liberation theology should be the concrete life situation of the oppressed people. This is precisely why when James Cone begins to list the fronts of theology, he begins by listing the experience, the history and culture of the Black people rather than begin with scripture. Similarly, a Santal Theology of Liberation must be based on the hard fact of Santal reality. It must start from the deep rooted experience of Santal oppression. It is from there we must begin analyzing the social realities and re-create the Bible and re-express our faith and thus re-create a theology that serves as a liberating force in creating a new Santal world. "It is not what are called 'evangelical values' that give meaning to social praxis. Quite the opposite is the case. Social praxis gives meaning to the former. Only this approach will enable the theology to get beyond the subject-object distortion that characterizes the present ideal character of Christianity"[28] retorts J.P. Richard.

Theology is a reflection on life. A Santal Theology of Liberation therefore, necessarily should grow out of a Santal oppressiveness...from Santal Christian soil. The Vatican-II decree on the Church's missionary activity is of the same view:

> The seed which is the word of God grows out of good soil watered by the divine dew, it absorbs moisture, transforms it, and makes it part of itself, so that evantually it bears much fruit. So too indeed, just as happened in the economy of the incarnation, the foundations of the apostles, take over all the riches of the nations which have been given to Christ (Ps. 2 : 8). They borrowed from the customs, traditions, wisdom, teaching, arts and sciences of their people everything which could be used to prasie the glory of the saviour, or contribute to the right ordering of Christian life"
>
> (Ad. Gentes Divinitus. no : 22)

The seed that is the word of must sprout and spread roots and prosper in our own soil. That indeed is the incarnation in its real sense. To this effect, the Gaudium et Spes reiterates, "Theology is fostering vital contact and exchange between the Church and different cultures" (G.S. on:44). The first letter of St. Paul to the Corinthians affirms this :

> "For though I am free from all men, I have made myself a slave of all, that I might win the more. To the Jews I became as a Jew, in-order to win Jews; to those under the law I became as one under the law...........that I might win those under the law. To those out-side the law I became as one out-side the law so that I might win whose out-side the law. To the weak I became weak that I might win the weak...." (1 Cor. 9 ; 19-25).

Surprisingly inspite of the decrees that there are in the Vatican Document, inspite of the model set by the apostles in the early Church, above all Jesus himself being the supreme model of incarnation, the Santal Church still remains alien to its soil...

non-ecclesiogenesis. Christianity as rightly pointed-out by Gerald Anderson, has been largely a "potted plant" in Santal—Parganas, transplanted without being transplanted.

So, if the Santal Church is to be relevant to the Santals today, it must necessarily possess a theology of its own that leads her people out of bondage to the land 'flowing with milk and honey'.........that which affect every sphere of its existence and activities. It must have structure and liturgy over-toning liberation and inculturation (appendix—6).

Conclusion

"As Christians", says Tom Driver, "Our first concern should be neither Christ not the Bible but the world of God."[29] This exactly is the deep concern of our theology. The Santals have been tragically expolited by the 'diku' land-lords, money-lenders and by the Indian government from the time of their settlement in the land of Saont. The Santals who were once masters of the jungle are made a 'non-people' by oppressive elements. They see death whenever they see a 'diku' Mahajon or money-lender. It is time for them to rise up to their human dignity...to be gospel-creators and not gospel-consumers. They believe in the word of God that is history shaking and history shaping. (By belief is meant to live accordingly). And their knowledge of Christ must come to them while they work out tehir liberation with him. But incase Christ comes to them in the form of a 'diku' Mahajon, money-lender or an exploiting government official they will not hesitate to get rid of him.

In this sense, James Cone explains prayers as "the spirit that evident in all the oppressed communities when they know that they have a job to do. It is the communication with the divine that makes them know that they have little to lose in the fight against evil and a lot to gain"[30]. The historical Jesus did not busy him-self offering libations and holocausts, rather he offered the oppressed hope while vehemenly condemning their oppressors. "Prayer is not a first thing a person does. Before praying, one experiences an existential shock. Only then does prayer pour forth, whether in form of supplication, or of an act of thanks-giving, or of worship"[31]. The worship God desires is one of justice and liberation of the oppressed, not any cultic form of worship. In this way only we can speak of Jesus' social commitment being a deep religious experience for him.

Though an utopian Santal world is eschatological, it "must focus on human beings (the Santals) as they exist in their existential situation, in which the meaning of history is located in the present moment of decision"[32]. The need of the hour for the Santal Church first and foremost is to inculturate her-self in Santal soil. This inculturation would necessarily mean joining hands with all secular forces that are struggling to liberate the oppressed Santals. The priestly training of the Santal Church therefore, should necessarily be oriented towards this new and challenging vision.

Notes

1. Malcom X. By any Means Necessary, George Breitman ed. (New York : Pathfinder Press, 1970). p. 155.
2. Indian Civil Service Documents, 1910.
3. Cone, James H. A Black Theology of Liberation. New York : Orbis Books, 1984. p. 1.
4. O'Grady, John F. Christian Anthropology. U.S.A. : Paulist Press, 1976. p. 100.
5. Fichtner, Joseph, O.S.C. Man the image of God. New York : Abba House, 1978. p. 35.
6. O'Grady, Christian Anthropology. p. 11.
7. Butter Worth Robert, S.J. The Theology of Creation. Cork : The Mercier Press, 1969. p. 84.
8. Gutierrez, Gustavo. A Theology of Liberation. London : SCM Press Ltd., 1983. p. 155.
9. Ibid. p. 231.
10. Ibid. p. 296.
11. Sobrino, John, S.J. Christology at the Cross-Road. London : SCM Press Ltd., 1978. p. 124.
12. Heschel, Abraham J. The Prophets. New York : Harper and Row Publishers., Inc., 1962. p. 5.

13. Hunter A.M. The work and words of Jesus. London : SCM Press, 1971. p. 61.
14. Fichtner. Man the image of God, p. 65.
15. Gutierrez. A Theology of Liberation, pp. 36-37.
16. Sartre, The Age of Reason, trans. by Eric Sutton (New York : Bantam Books, 1968), p. 135.
17. Ellacuria, Ignacio. Freedom made flesh. New York : Orbis Books, 1976. p. 216.
18. Lonergan, "Insight Revisited", in second collection, London, 1974, pp. 276-7.
19. Avila, Rafael. Worship and Polities. New York : Orbis Books, 1981. p. 30.
20. Ellacuria, Freedom made flesh, p. 246.
21. Segundo, Juan Louis. The Liberation of Theology. New York : Orbis Books, 1977. p. 74.
22. Ellacuria, 1976, p. 162.
23. Segundo, 1977, p. 97.
24. Gutierrez. A Theology of Liberation, p. 11.
25. Ellacuria, Freedom made flesh, p. 116.
26. Ibid, p. 198.
27. Segundo, 1977, p. 65.
28. Driver, Tom F. Christ in a changing world. London : SCM Press Ltd., 1981. p. 83.
29. Cone, A Black Theology of Liberation, p. 133.
30. Boff Leonardo. Jesus Christ Liberator. Great Britain: Biddles Ltd., Gildford and King's Lynn, 1987. p. 10.
31. Cone, A Black Theology of Liberation, p. 138.

APPENDICES

Appendix I

NEHRU'S TRIBAL PANCHESHEEL

1. The people should develop along the lines of their own genius and we should avoid imposing anything on them. We shold try to encourage them in every way in the preservation of their own traditional arts and culture.

2. Tribal Rights in land and forests shold be respected.

3. We shold try to train and build up a team of their own people to participate in administration and development. Some technical personnel from outside will, no doubt, be nedded especially in the beginning. But we should avoid introducing too many outsiders into tribal territory.

4· We should not over-administer these areas or over-burden them with a multiplicity of schemes. We should rather work through and not in rivalry with their own social and cultural institutions

5. We should judge results not by statistics nor by the amount of money spent but by the quality of human character that is evolved.

Appendix II

DAK' BAP'LA MYTH

There lived a Santal farmer who had four children—three girls and a boy. Once on a sunny morning, he went out to his field to plough it. Reaching the field that was far off from home he realized he had forgotten to take the yoke along. He was ashamed of himself and he did not want to go home to bring it in that scorching heat. So, he sat under a tree brooding over his foolishness. Wanting to take advantage of the situation, a tiger came along and promised to lend him an yoke on the condition that the farmer gave his eldest daughter in marriage to him. The man agreed, got the yoke and ploughed his land. At dusk he returned the yoke and promised the tiger that he would sent his eldest daughter to the far off pond that evening itself as he was instructed.

Regretting the promise he had made and gripped by the fear of being eatten up by the tiger if he were to break the promise, the farmer returned home. Standing outside his house, all full of mud, he called out to his eldest daughter and asked her to fetch him water from the pond so that he could wash himself. As it was already dark, the girl persisted and asked him to go over to the pond and take a dip. On his insistance with much hesitation and irritation, the girl agreed to fetch him water from that pond. As she was about to go, her little brother insisted on his aceompanying her. As no amount of reason could reproach him, she agreed to take him along. As it was dark, he as any other Santal boy, took a bow and a couple of arrows in hand. Approaching the pond, the boy aimed an arrow at a bird sitting on a tree. To their surprise, the arrow hit the eye of the tiger that was waiting for her beside the pond. And it ran for life.

With gladdened heart the girl dipped the pot in the pond, filled it with water and lifted it on her head. As they walked back home, the girl noticed a long thread leech linking her water-pot to the pond. Taken aback, she kept the pot on the ground for a while hoping the leech would detach itself of the pot. For a while it did, but as soon as the girl took the pot on her head it resumed its link. Suspecsing her father's intention, she left the pot there and went way to the neighbouring village to her aunt's house taking her brother along.

The farmer regretfully accepted the misfortune that fell on the girl but was very worried about the disappearance of the boy. Keeping all in secret he went all over looking for the boy; And finally, he went over to his sister's house. His sister called him in and asked him in detail of the misfortune that fell on him. The girl and her little brother hid themselves and listened as he narrated the story. Then they came out and told their father how mean he had been with his own children and they refused to be called his children. The man wept bitterly, asked pardon and promised to give the girl in solemn marriage to a beautiful boy living next to their village. Thus he won them back.

Appendix III

TARWARDI BAP'LA MYTH

This myth is inter-linked with 'dak' bap'la' myth. The farmer arranged a solemn wedding for his eldest daughter. On the day of the marriage, as the bride's party was getting ready for 'daram dak'', they realized there was not a doop of water left in the house. So the mother of the bride rushed to the nearby well to fetch water for the ritual. As she began drawing water from the well, the rope snaped and the pot fell into the well. Turning around she saw a snake sitting beside the well and it wouldn't allow her to move away from the well. Fceling desparate, the lady asked the snake what it wanted. The snake said that it would allow her to draw water from the well only if she gave her eldest daughter in marriage to him. The lady agreed to do so. On her return, the news spread like wild fire. Hearing of this bad omen, the groom's party was upset. But the shrewd women-folk of the village quietly plotted against the snake and approached their men for help. As their men folk were drunk and were sleeping, they sought the help of the 'doms', the drummers. They dressed two young girls of the village as bride and her helper and went dancing to the well with sword, bows and arrows. On reaching the well they told the snake that had come ready for the marriage that he should allow them to perform all their traditional rituals and dances before that and that he should lie quietly beside the well till they finished them all. The sanke initially resisted, but at their insistance it agreed. So after having performed the ritual invoking the blessings of their ancestors at the well, the women folk began dancing around the well pointing the 'tarward' and arrows to the ground while the drummers blasted their drums. And when the snake lay dazed with the violent drum beat and dancing, the women-folk stabbed it, hit it and killed it. Having won victory over the evil one, the snake, they filled the pots with water, returned home in joyful dance and showed the blood tainted sword to the bride in assurance of their victory over the evil one (therefore a good omen), and gave her a bath with the water they brought from the well.

Appendix IV

KANṬHAR BUṬA ẠṚ BIḌẠK′ REAK′ BIṄTI

Sạriạt mạṅjhi do galmaraoe ehoba :

E baba Bạriạtko, mit́ bar kathabon galmaraoange. Sendrare se karkare; ạhnire muhnire bol kạbul do baṅ kana; tobe etom uṛić koṅe ere sarket́ sạgunket́te sikṛiak′ mạkṛiak′bo tol mit́ hel mit́ket́abo; tobe siṅ boṅga buru mõṛẽ mare hapṛamko duṛup′kate sikṛiak′ mạkṛiak′bo tol mit́ hel mit́ket́abo. Teheṅ khon bạhu seć reak′ oṛak′ do jãwãe doe ṅamkeda, arejãwãe seć reak′ oṛak′ do bạhui ṅamkeda, ado oṛak′ utiṅge hoyena. Ado jãhã leka sendra karkape daṛana, jãhã leka haṭ baṭpe calak′a, gã gonḍape dãṛãna, tobe nin din do ajante sut́ dak′ ḍạḍi dak′pe ṅukeda, nõk′õe teheṅ do oṛak′bon kiriṅkeda, teheṅ khon do ado alope etom koṅea. Ado oṛak′ umulrege mit́ basna dak′ ar goṛa umul, nia bare hećak′pe. Nõk′õe ape do gelbar awa khon bhajanpe bachaokeda, ṭhukiạ bạjiạkatepe kiriṅkeda; ado kuṛhiạk′ kan bhaṅgṛaok′ kan, kãṛãk′ kan khõṛẽk′ kan, gaṛhak′ kan sotok′ kan, aleak′ elaka do bạnuk′anaṅ—raṅok′ kan tambak′ kan, dạrik′ kan chinạrok′ kan, ranok′ kan naṅjomok′ kan, baba, ape satatege calak′a. Oṛak′ gunạk′ hoṛko benaok′a, goṛa gunạk′ gạiko benaok′a—gonoṅ ṭaka hõle jom unumkeda, bare itạt́, jiạ itạt́, eṅga itạt́ inạko sańamle jom unumkeda, bare itạt́, jiạ itạt́, eṅga itạt́ inạko sanamle jom unumkeda. Jaṅ hō jaṅ toroć hō toroćle ạkriṅkeda menkhan baba, bohok' mãyãm lutur mãyãm inạ do baṅle ạkrin' akada. Ona dole pańjae gea. Tobe nin din tara din daka roṅgok' utu roṅgok' do sahaoke lahaoape : Sikhạu sikhạu paṛhao paṛhaote baṅ jutlenre, phalna mạńjhi baba, mit́ṭen hoṛ baṛe kolalepe, hoṛ bako ńamok' khan mit́ goṭen laḍea ṭheṅga baṛe kolalepe ar enkan ṭheṅga hō baṅ ńamok' khan mit́ṭen kaṛyo kaṛyo seta hō kolalepe, adobon cepet́a arbon bupujhạua.

Enka aṅjom purạukate Bạriạt mạńjhie roṛ ruạṛa :

Hẽge phalna mạńjhi saheb, sạrige noa ma abote ma baṅa, siń boṅga buru mõṛẽ ar mare hapṛamko duṛup'kate etom uṛić, koye ere sarket́ sạgunket́te sikṛiak' makṛiak'bo joṛao keda. Sạrige, gelbar awa khon bhajan dole bachao keda, ṭhukiạ bạjiạkate jinisle kiriṅkeda. Ṭena miru do apeak' ṭena khon aleak' ṭenatele ucạṛkedea; ado raṅok' kan tambak' kan, alerenge hoṛ do kuṛhiạk' kan bhạṅgṛạk' kan ale satatege calak'a. Gaṛhaok' kan sotok' kan ona hō ale satatege calak'a. Khalok' kan ḍobok' kan ona hō ale satatege calak'a. Dạrik' kan chinạrok' kan, ranok' kan naṅjomok kan ale satatege calak'a. Kombṛok' kan bokṛok' kan inạ hō ale satatege calak'a. Jaṅ ho jaṅ toroć hō toroć teheń dole kiriṅkeda. Bohok' mãyãm ar lutur mãyãm inạ do bale kiriń akada, ona dope pańja daṛeak'a. Hẽ tobe, mit́ din tara din, daka roṅgok utu roṅgok unre do babo sikhạu paṛhaoea ? Ar bae sikhạuk paṛhaok' khan ape ṭhen katha koltebon cepet́a. Hẽ tobe ape hō jãhã leka ale sećpe calak'a, alope etom koṅelea. Sendra karka, gã goṇḍa morod bhãorape daṛana alope etom koṅea. Nin din do ajante sut́ dak' dạḍi dak'pe ńukeda, teheń khon do ona do hō kak' karekak'pe. Jhata umul tmbạ dak' baṛe sohor seṭerak'pe. Nenḍenak' oṛak' do aleak' ar hanḍenak' oṛak' do apeak' kangea.

TRANSLATION

'Kanṭhaṛ buṭa'[1] *and farewell deliberations*

The 'Sạriạt'[3] headman will start the eoversation :

'E baba[4] bạriạtko',[2] let us converse a few words.

Neither at the chase and hunt nor by virtue of hypnotism or assurance but having got a good omen from an 'urić'[5] on the right and an 'ere'[6] on the left we have solemnised this marriage. At the behest of the Sun God and five old ancestors we have contracted this marriage. From this day onwards the bride's home will belong to the groom and the groom's to the bride—this accomplishes the exchange of the houses. If per chance, you go out for the chase and hunt, move out to the market place, villages and hamlets, so long a time you have, because we were not known to each other, drunk water from hollowed out cavity or from a pool but henceforth as we have bought this house do not go else where; but do frequent this house for a glass of cool water and serene shelter. You have selected it out of twelve kilns by tapping and sounding. Now whether it (she) be lame or blind, fair or dark, idle or idiot we do not have our whereabouts. Whether it turns out to be pewter or copper, witch or whore, medicine or potion it will go the way you wish. A man is identified by virtue of the house he lives in and a cow by its cowshed. The 'Gonoń ṭaka'[7] has been finished off; and 'bare itạt́,[8] jiạ itạt́,[9] eṅga itạt́'[10] have all been exhausted too. We have sold off everything in its totality, body and soul, but not blood; that we will surely follow up. In future if after repeated advise and teaching it falls to amend itself, you the mạńjhi baba do send us a messenger, in his non-availability do send us two crooked staff representing him, and if that too is not available send a black dog, then we will discuss and reconcile.

After hearing the bạriạt mạn'jhi will respond:

Right, Mạn'jhi saheb, verily this has not been through us but on the behest of the Sun God and five old ancestors and because of the good omen of 'uric'' on the right and 'ere' bird on the left we have solemnised this marriage. Truly, we have bought it out of twelve kilns after tapping and sounding. We have removed your tame parrowkeet from its stand to ours.

So whether it be pewter or copper it is ours; idle or idiot it will accompany us; fair or dark it will accompany us; broken or brittle it will accompany us. Whether witch or whore, medicine or potion it will come with us; whether it be thief, it too will be with us. We have bought it in its entirety but have spared its blood. This we have not bought. That you can follow. So, shall we not teach and advise when there is anything wrong in cooking? And verily in failing to learn and listen we will send a message to you and reconcile.

You too, when you go our way, do not go elsewhere. If per chance you go out for the chase and hunt, move out to the villages and hamlets do not go elsewhere. So long a time you have, because we were not known to each other drunk water from a hollowed out cavity or from a pool from today onwards leave it off. But do frequent this house for a glass of water and for serene shelter. The house here is ours and the one there is yours.

Foot Note :

1. Meeting of the elders of 'bariat, and 'sariat' at bride's village.
2. Bride-groom's party.
3. The male members of bride's village whe go out to meet the bride-groom's party.
4. Respectful address to the elders.

5. A tiny bird.
6. A tiny bird.
7. Bride price.
8. A bullock given at the time of marriage by the bride-groom to the bride's brothers.
9. The grand-mother's portion at the marriage of her grand-daughter.
10. A cloth given at the time of marriage to the bride's mother by the bride-groom.

Appendix V

SANTAL CLANS AND MAJOR SUB-CLANS

I. KISKU (Raja)
lived in
Champa nagar

1. Nij Kisku
2. gaṛ Kisku
3. Ok′ Kisku
4. Ober Kisku
5. Mańjhi Khil Kisku
6. Naeke Khil Kisku
7. Son Kisku
8. Aḍ Kisku
9. Badar Kisku
10. Biṭal Kisku
11. sada Kisku
12. Paṭi Kisku
13. Jabe Kisku
14. Ṭika Kisku
15. Katwa Kisku

II. TUḌU (Mantharia)
lived in
Duisanagar gaṛ

1. Nij Ṭudu
2. Cigi Ṭudu
3. Lat́ Ṭudu

4. mańjhikhil Ṭudu
5. Naeke khil ,,
6. Sada Ṭudu
7. gaṛ Ṭudu
8. Jugi Ṭudu
9. Dantela Ṭudu
10. ok' Ṭudu
11. Biṭal Ṭudu
12. ober Ṭudu
13. Baske Ṭudu
14. Tilok Ṭudu
15. Babṛen Ṭudu
16. Curuć Ṭudu
17. Kuḍam Ṭudu
18. Bhokta Ṭudu
19. Kharhara Ṭudu

III. MARANDI (Kipisãṛ) lived in Ajodhiya gaṛ

1. Nij Maranḍi
2. goda maranḍi
3. Mańjhi Khil maranḍi
4. Naeke khil ,,
5. Rot maranḍi
6. Rok' lutur maranḍi
7. Ober maranḍi
8. Biṭol maranḍi
9. Sidup' maranḍi
10. Jugi maranḍi
11. Kaḍa maranḍi
12. gaṛ maranḍi
13. Khara maranḍi
14. Kulkhi maranḍi

15. Turko lumam maranḍi
16. Sada maranḍi
17. Khanḍa jagao maranḍi
18. Ṭika maranḍi
19. Ponḍ maranḍi
20. Keḍwaṛ maranḍi
21. Buru bereṭ maranḍi
22. Khanda maranḍi
23. Babṛen maranḍi
24. Rupa maranḍi
25. Jonok′ maranḍi
26. Miru maranḍi
27. Bhose maranḍi

IV. HEMBROM (Hende meromko) Bir kali Pujai tahen lived in Pouwagulin gaṛ

1. Ṇij Hembrom
2. mańjhi khil Hembrom
3. naeke khil
4. Sada Hembrom
5. Biṭal Hembrom
6. gua Hembrom
7. gua soren Hembrom
8. Ober Hembrom
9. Badaṛ Hembrom
10. gaṛ Hembrom
11. Laher Hembrom
12. Casa Hembrom
13. Hanḍi Hembrom
14. Sole Hembrom
15. Ṭhakur Hembrom
16. Laṭ Hembrom
17. Datela Hembrom
18. Kuanri Hembrom

V. SOREN (sipahi) were not allotted any particultar area 'Barchi' is the main source to have their shelter and living any where.

1. nij Soren
2. Sidup' Soren
3. Sada Soren
4. Jugi Seren
5. mańjhi Khil Soren
6. Naehe Khil Soren
7. Biṭol Soren
8. OK' Soren
9. munḍu/Badar Soren
10. mal Soren
11. Jiḥu Soren
12. Sank Soren
13. Barchi Soren
14. Sada Sidup' Soren
15. Panḍ Soren
16. Khanḍan Soren
17. Obor Seron
18. manṛ Soren
19. Cehel Soren
20. Dantela Soren
21. Rek' butur Soren
22. gua Soren
23. Turku lumam Soren.

VI. MURMU (takur) lived in Saragpuri gaṛ

1. nij Murmu
2. Sada murmu
3. Obor Murmu
4. mańjhi khil murmu
5. naeke khil murmu
6. Biṭal murmu
7. gaṛ murmu

8. Badar murmu
9. ok′ murmu
10. laṭ murmu
11. Jihu murmu
12. Tika/Tilok murmu
13. Kuḍam murmu
14. Gajaṛ murmu
15. Copiar murmu
16. Ponḍ murmu
17. Boara murmu
18. Handi murmu
19. Koṭha murmu
20. Ṭuṭi sarjom murmu
21. Samak′ saṅ murmu
22. Oara murmu
23. munḍu murmu
24. Jugi murmu
25. Kaḍa murmu
26. Turku Lumam murmu
27. Sau murmu
28. Powar murmu

VII. HANSDAK′ (Hasa boṅga) : lived in Tati Jhari gaṛ

1. Nij Hembram
2. Manjhi khil Hembram
3. Naeke khil Hembram
4. Sada Hembram
5. Biṭol Hembram
6. Gua Hembram
7. Gua soren Hembram
8. Obor Hembram
9. Badaṛ Hembram
10. Gaṛ Hembram

11. Laher Hembram
12. Casa Hembram
13. Handi Hembram
14. Sole Hembram
15. Thakur Hembram
16. Lat́ Hembram
17. Datela Hembram
18. Kuanri Hembram

VIII. BESRA (Nachonia) lived in Bethl nagar gaṛ

1. Nij Besra
2. Man'jhi khil Besra
3. Naeke khil Besra
4. Kuhi Besra
5. Son Besra
6. Bindaṛ Besra
7. Gaṛ Besra
8. Tilok Besra
9. Biṭol Besra
10. Lat́ Besra
11. Baske Besra
12. Ok' Besra
13. Obor Bessa
14. Kãhu Besra

IX. CHORE (Donaiya Guru/Tirio oroṅ guru): lived in Gagichowri area.

1. Nij Chõṛe
2. Gua Chõṛe
3. Hembram kunar cõṛe
4. Gua Hembram cõṛe
5. Sada cõṛe
6. Biṭol cõṛe
7. Man'jhikhil cõṛe
8. Ok' cõṛe

9. Gaṛ cõṛe
10. Naeke khil cõṛe
11. Sindur cõṛe
12. Bindaṛ cõṛe
13. Kãhu cõṛe
14. Laṭ cõṛe
15. Ṭhakur cõṛe

X. BASKEY (Kakoe hoṛ) :

1. Nij Baske
2. Man'jhi khil Baske
3. Naeke khil Baske
4. Biṭol Baske
5. Kuhi Baske
6. Ok'' Baske
7. Munḍu Baske
8. Obor Baske
9. Bindaṛ Baske
10. Sada Baske
11. Keḍwar Baske
12. Jihu Baske
13. Sãru Gaḍa Baske
14. Bhiḍi Baske
15. Suṛe Baske
16. Hende Baske

XI. PAURIA : lived in Setapuri-Para pachit area.

1. Nij Pauria
2. Mańjhi khil Pauria
3. Naeke khil Pauria
4. Sada Pauria
5. Ok' Pauria
6. Cauria Pauria
7. Bhitar Pauria
8. Obor Pauria

9. Sidup' Pauria
10. Biṭol Pauria
11. Gaṛ Pauria
12. Mundu Pauria
13. Laṫ Pauria

XII. GANDWER/BEDEA : lived in Diyan buru area.	Only a handful of Santals belonging to this clan are found around Laṛbathan in Sahibganj district.

Appendix VI

Church organization play a vital role in bringing Christ's vision to realization. Dealing with the church and her mission in the santal home-land in this chapter draws our attention to the response of social Development centre, Dumka to the challenges that the Santal church is faced with.

Social Development Centre : *Its response* : Social Development Centre (S.D.C.), founded in september, 1981 is the diocesan pastoral centre, coordinating in an integrated way the various apostolates and activities of the Catholic diocese of Dumka (Bihar). The centre has the Head-offices of five main Departments of work, namely, Faith Formation, Education, Community Health Care, Socio-economic Development and Multi-media Communications. Each of these Departments is headed by a qualified person who is ably assisted by an average of five animators. The Director of the Centre Fr. Kisar Kiru (Richard), who is also the Master-Mind behind it, is the over-all coordinator of these Departments.

In these few pages I intend to highlight briefly the sincere efforts made by S.D.C. to liberate the oppressed Santals from multiple angles of life and how it is an agent of God's kingdom in Dumka diocese.

A. **Socio-Economic Development Department**

Started in 1982, the Socio-economic Development has made sincere efforts to remedy the situation with particular attention to the following fields :

a. *Legal Education programme* :

Caught in the cob-web of law-courts, the ordinary villager has been fighting a losing battle. To rescue him from such a bondage, the Centre launched Legal Education Programme (L.E.P). So far it has been able to train barefootlawyers and trainers like village-leaders, Social-workers and School-teachers...a cadre of 200 motivated men and women. The Programme dwells on problems of land and the ways to reclaim land-holdings lost to greedy money-lenders.

b. *Agro-Service Programme* :

Short-term training courses and demonstrations are being orgainsed in improved methods of cultivation and water-harvesting. Proper use of fertilisers and pesticides and choice of hybrid seeds for better cropping have been taught profitably at the Centre followed up in the villages. A revolving fund for purchase of seeds and fertilisers as well as for community stocking has been made available to very deserving farmers. Through Food-Work and Cash-projects, dugwells, water tanks and small water-sheds have been constructed to the optimum benefit of farmers who have been organised into 'Ebhen Baisies'.

c. *Seri-culture & Afforestation* :

With the help and assistance of the local government the centre has been able to motivate and train several villagers in sericulture. Several acres of land lying fallow for so many years have turned green with mulbari tree plantation to raise silk-worms. Approaching the local government officers. It has been trying to dig wells for proper irrigation of the seedlings.

In order to arrest erosion of land lying alongside rivulets, several villagers have been encouraged to plant trees which as well helps to induce monsoon rains on a regular basis.

d. *Grain Banks & Small Saving Scheme* :

Santals economy is in kind; it is only of late that they have been introduced to cash-economy. As improvident people, the Santal tribals have been living from hand to mouth without saving for lean days as well as for the health care and education of their children. Cocerted efforts have been made by the centre's Social animators to motivate and educate people to save both in kind and cash on a regular basis.

e. *Pump-set & Vocational Training* :

Out in the villages pump-sets with the Government Subsidy have been made use of by even average farmers. School dropouts and rural youth have been encouraged since a couple of years now to undergo a 3 month-training course in Pump-set repairing as well as other skills like cycle-re-pairing, tailoring and driving. Started in a humble way, these programmes have given rise to a Vocational Training Institute near the Centre under construction at present.

f. *Community Cluster Programme* :

'Ebhen Baisi' is the cluster approach to community development. Each cluster consists of 5—9 villages organised for community development programmes. Concerted efforts are being made by all departments in these clusters. For the under-fives 'Balwadi' pre-schools have been started, and village-schools are numbering now 60 for the older ones; 'grihini' programmes have been taken up for marriageable groups of girls at different sub-centres numbering 16 in all, and vocational and agricultural training courses for boys. Aperiod of conscientization precedes each of these programmes.

B. **Cmmunity Health Care Department (CHC)**

(i) *Community Health Workers* (*CHW*) :

In an effort to carry health education and medical care right down to villages, since 1983 the CHC Dept. of the Centre has been orgainsing community Health Workers' training courses for women of different villages. Health and hygene, basic principles of good health, first aid, home remedies, balance diet, nutrition and safe drinking water have been much emphasised upon. Over a 100 CHWS have so far trained and these are placed under the super-vision of Registered Nurses (RNMS) in 16 Health Centres these review the field-work as well receive more inputs on health-related issues.

(ii) *Community Health Animators* (*CHA*) :

Some among the Health workers have been selected for further training to the Community Health Centre and the community of villages. The CHAs also help at various clinics and health education programmes like, ante natal, post natal, and mother-and-child care programmes etc. There are about 12 such CHAs full-time engaged in such programmes.

(iii) *Local Birth Attendants* :

It has been the common practice in the tribal villages for an ordinary unqualified women to assist at deliveries. Trial and error methods of these women called 'DAIS' locally have endangered lives of mothers and of infants at birth due to unhygenic and unscientific handling of delivery cases. Because they are trusted by village people the Centre has recruited these traditional midwives for short-term course and try to correct their mistakes and provide some basic guidance so as to handle deliveries safe and refer those that are difficult to the Health Centres or hospitals.

(iv) *Kala-azar Control Programme* :

Along the Gangetic plains of Sahibganj district, black-fever commonly known here as 'kala-azar' has taken a heavy toll of simple and ordinary people susceptible to the bites of sand-flies. Enlargement of spleen accompanied by high fever and headache are its symptoms. Men, women and even infants are prone to it. With financial assistance from some donors we have so far been able to treat 6000 cases to safety. This the Centre has been doing successfully with the help of paramedicals trained at its Health Centres of Kindly, Mariampahar and Sahibganj.

(v) *School Health Programme* :

Teachers and children can be motivated to become agents of promoting community health. In this regard, the Centre has successfully introduced school health education Programme in its primary, middle and high-schools. From the Centre, the Health Team goes out to each school to conduct short courses for teachers accomapnied by practical sessions with students. The promising students are picked out to impart health education to the younger ones. And, finally from teacher student approach and child-to-child health care, our focus has been turned to school-to-village community healh care programme. The first step has already been taken.

(vi) *Care of Physically Handicapped Children* :

While the CHC department of the Centre has taken up immunization for children in a systematic way, care is also being taken of polio victims physically handicapped and incapacitated to a normal life by the CPHC. With the consent of Parents, such children are admitted into physio-theropeutic clinics for surgery and caliper fittings. Those who went hopping come back walking—this is the miracle of loving care !

C. Primary Education Department

In response to the problems faced by the ordinary people, particulary by the tribal community of our area, the programme of Village Primary Schools was launched by the Centre. Over 60 schools were instituted at various villages where people wanted their children to be educated. Today over 7000 children receive education in their own villages and local tribal teachers have been motivated through inservice-training courses to make school life an experience for young students.

(a) *Head-mistresses' Meeting* :

Twice every year, meetings is being held for all the Head-mistresses of the Centre's schools to plan out the years programme for their respective schools as well as to evaluate their performance as per plan of action for the year.

b. *Teachers' Training Courses* :

Almost every quarter of the year, teachers are encouraged to attend on-going motivation and animation courses at the Centre in different subjects of the School curriculum. Value-education is a necessary component of such training courses. Teaching aids are also provided to each school.

c. *School Visitations* :

The Central Staff make periodic visits to all the schools under their supervision to check on the lesson-plans and teaching methods of teachers as a follow-up. Further inputs and suggestions for improvements in the quality of teaching and the general discipline of the schools are given. On such occasions the staff meeting is also held for encouragement.

d. *Animation of Government School Teachers* :

While the Centre runs its own schools as best as it could, sincere attempt is also made to inspire teachers engaged in the neighbourhood Government-run schools to attend classes regularly as well as to make schooling attractive for students.

e. *Teachers' Annual Get-together* :

Every year all the teachers of the Centre have a 5 day programme of spiritual renewal and social awareness. As elites in their respective areas, our teachers are exported and encouraged to live exemplary lives for ordinary people to emulate as well as to provide enlightened leadership to local village communities on development lines.

f. *Village-School Managing Committees* :

In an attempt to promote emerging local leader-ship from among the people so as to take responsibility for the running and general management of the primary and middle schools, School Managing Committees are being formed. Special training courses are being organised for the Committee members to orientate them to the necessity of basic education of children as well as to encourage community involvement in the process of such an education.

g. *Talent Hunt* :

The School Department of the Centre continues to make the child as the focal-point of all its efforts, making the School itself as an agent of socio-spiritual change. Inter-school competitions in sports and cultural items, picnics for educational exposures, skills-training courses and small-saving schemes are some of the interesting initiatives introduced to make the school, indeed an attraction.

h. *Healthy Infra-structure* :

Whereas nearly 1000 primary schools in the State of Bihar are running without a teacher and over 13,000 schools are single-teacher schools, the Centre has been able to provide well-motivated and dedicated teachers to all its schools. While more than 40% of the State-run primary schools do not have any building at all, the buildings of another 20% are in a dilapidated condition, and less than 1% of the total 63,000 primary schools enjoy the facilities of furniture, toilet, drinking-water and games, the Centre has been making systematic efforts to provide its schools with decent buildings, toilet-blocks and for safe-drinking water, bore-wells.

(i) *A.E.A. Sponsorship Programme* :

Wherever local government facilities are available, the Centre has encouraged its schools to benefit by the same like subsidies and stipends for tribal children of lower-income families. Meanwhile, much of our success to implement the aforesaid programmes has been possible by the generous contributions made by the Aide et Action, an organization that encourages donors to sponsor the children. This however, involve a lot of desk work which the Centre takes care of.

D. **Faith-formation Deptt.**

The department of Faith-formation strives to build up Basic Christian Communities as core-groups at the service of entire village communities. In this direction, attention has been given to the following aspects:

(i) *Marriage Preparation Courses* :

Young boys and girls engaged for marriage are brought together for a fortnight training course to become responsible couples. Inter-personal communication and relationships are topics of interest besides responsible parenthood like child bearing and child-rearing according to the modern trends in psychology.

(ii) *Marriage Renewal/Encounter* :

Short-tem courses for such couples are organised periodically to review nuptial life and problems of interpersonal relationships as well as to provide married couples greater motivation for unconditional love and marital fidelity. Lessons are also conducted in child and teenage psychology to cope up with the challenges of changing times and behaviour patterns of present day children.

(iii) *Family Catechises* :

In view of building a healthy local church, strengthening of Catholic family life has been felt most urgent. In this regard the Department of Faith-formation has been organising at parish level seminars for couples to strengthen family ties promote family prayer and foster vocations among children.

(iv) *Charismatic Renewal Programmes* :

Since 1985 with the help of Dumkais Religional Centre, Patna (BIHAR) the Centre was able to introduce the priests, religious and lay-leaders of Dumka to Charismatic Renewal programmes. Back in the diocese too, followed up the Renewal with retreats, seminars and training of parish Charismatic retreat teams. As a result, in so many different villages several retreats have been preached to strengthen the Christian people in the faith so as to make them evangelisers of their follow-men and women.

(v) *Home Cell Groups/Basic Christian Communities* :

Following the efforts of village Charismatic Retreat Teams, steps are being taken to organise at several villages cells of 10-15 families for Bible-reflection and prayer-sharing. This is to strengthen the faith of the cell-members as well as to encourage them to share their faith-experience with non-Christian neighbours so as to lead individuals or entire families to Christ.

(vi) *Catholic Women's Association* (*Mahila Sangh*) :

Catholic women in each of the Centre's parishes are well organised on socio-spiritual lines to work for all-round development of their village communities. At the diocesan level there is a full-timer at the Centre to animate and coordinate the parish 'Mahila Sangh' units. Women are made aware of their right place in society and in the Church to play their role as evangelizers and family-builders. Every year, the Catholic Women's Association has its Diocesan Rally to discuss and decide on a big way the thrusts of their work.

(vii) *Inter-diocesan Programmes* :

The Santal people being the largest homogeneous tribe in India, 8 million forming 1% of India's total population, are found in 19 dioceses of India. In order there may be sharing of experiences and mutual learining from missionaries, the following inter-diocesan inter-actions have been a regular feature orgainsed by the Centre.

a. *Santal Indepth Studies* :

In order to understand the Santal, his personality, Value-system, socio-political infra-structure, local leadership styles, and religious beliefs and practices, since 1986 onwards indepth studies have been done by the Centre. This is primarily towards an effective communication of the Good-News' and the Kingdom Values' to the Santal Community respecting all that it holds in high esteem, in other words, such an effort is directed towards inculturation so as to incarnate the Church among this people.

b. *Santal Convention* :

Santal priests, religious and those in formation have an annual convention to discuss issues of importance to build up truely a local church among the Santals. Such a convention is primary to foster a deep sense of solidarity among the Santal Church personnel scattered all over, as well as to discern and suggest together to the Church authorities the best approaches to effective evangelisation of the people.

E. Social Communication Department

At the service of all the aforesaid Departments is the Social Communication department producing and providing training-cum teaching aids like charts, posters, film-strips, slides, photographs, cassettes, flannel-graphs, and such local and low-cost audio and video materials.

In short, the Social Development Centre was founded primarily to boost up the work of evangelization and catechesis through an integrated approach to man/woman in his/her totality......social and spiritual. Thus, the Centre, since 8th September 1981 has been initiating, animating, and coordin ating the efforts or the Dumka Catholic Church in the fields of Faith-formation, Primary Education, Community Health Care and Socio-economic Development. Each department at the diocesan level has its counter-part at the parish level too. A batch of 10 Community Centres were established to spearhead the integrated approach to evangelization. And, today, they are flourishing Catholic Centres with schools catering for about 7000 students, Health Units assisted by Regd. Nurses, Health workers, and Health Animators caring for the sick and the suffering in the remote villages. Charismatic Retreat Teams reaching out to so may villages of some Christian presence, and the Socio-economic programmes launched systematically for the all-round development of total village-communities. The contribution of the Centre, thus is vital for the development of the people of Santal Parganas.

Glossary

A

Apaṅgir bap'la	Marriage of the boy and girl who had illegal love-affair.

B

Baha	Flower, Female sex organ
Bạhu-bande	Draping the bride with saree
Balaea-johar	Greeting between the in-laws
Bandan	Death ceremony
Bap'la	Marriage, Wedding
Bhagats	A Hindu business class who exploit the Santals
Bir	Hill, Mountain
Biṭ-laha	Excommunication
Boka	Fool, Stupid
Boṅga	Spirit

Bariatok'	The journey of bride-groom's party to the bride's village.

C

Caco	Toddling
Caco-Chaṭiar	Initiation-rite
Chae-Champa	Land of five rivers, the place where the Santals originally settled in India
Chando-Baba	Sun-like God, The God Supreme
Chaṭiar	Rite

D

Daḥṛi	Turban
Dak'	Water
Dak'-bap'la	Water-marriage
Dak bangalow	Government rest-House
Dạn	Witch
Daram-dak'	A ceremony performed at the reception of the bride-groom's party at the outskirt of the bride's village.
Desh	Nation
Desh-Man'jhi	An assistant official to the Pargana
Dhuti	Dhoti—An Indian male dress
Diḥri	The hunt-priest

Diku	A non-Santal, an oppressor
Din	Day
Disom	Nation
Disom-Sendra	National-hunt
Docoitee	Looting, plundering

E

Era	Lady
Erok'	To sow
Erok-Sim	Sowing-Chicken
Gidi-Cumạuṛa	Waving ceremony
Gira-Tol	Date fixing ceremony
Godeṭ	Village announeer
Golaeṭi-bap'la	Inter marriage between two families in places of giving bride-price
Gonom	Bride-price
Guṛjom	Eating molases, the official visit of the groom's house-hold to all the houses in the village of the bride
Gossain' Era	One of the ladies of the grove (Spirit)
Guru	Teacher, Master

H

Hanapuri	The other world
Handi	Rice-beer

Hap'ṛamko	Ancestors
Hirom cetan bap'la	Marriage of a second wife
Horok' Cikhna	Dressing ceremony of the bride and the groom
Hoṛ	Man, Santal
Hoṛ-hopon	Son of Man, Santal
Hul	Rebellion, Revolt

I

Itut́-bap'la	Forced marriage by applying vermilion on the fore-head of a girl

J

Jaisim Boṅga	A major Super-natural spirit
Jamindar	Land-lord
Janam-Chaṭiar	Birth purificatory rite
Jan, Jan-Guru	Witch-finder
Jãwãe kirin' bap'la	Marriage by giving groom-price
Jãwãe Dhuti	Dressing the groom
Jom-hem	Widow, Widower
Jharkhand	Hill-strip
Jog	Sweep
Jog-Man'jhi	The village official who looks after the morals of the youth of the village
Jog-Paranik	An assistant to the head-man of the village

K

Kạmiya	Bonded-labourer
Kirin' bạhu bap'la	A bought bride marriage
Kudạm naeke	Assistant to the village priest
Kulhi-duṛup'	Village council
Kundal n'apam bap'la	Marriage by illicit connection
Kunṭi	Pole

L

Landa	Laugh, Joke
Landa-sạgại	Joking relation-ship
Liṭa	The God supreme, the grand-father who taught the Santals how to brew ricebeer
Lo-Bir	Burning-hill, Hill-council
Loṭa	Mug
Loṭa-dak'	Mug of water

M

Mag	To cut, month of Mag
Mag-Sim	Mag month chicken, a feast cele-brated in the month of Mag
Mahajon	Money-lender, Big man
Man'jhi	Head-man, Village head-man, leader
Mandu bap'la	Marriage by illicit connection
Mandwa	Marriage-shed

Mandwa-kunṭi — Marriage-shed-pole

Man jhi haṛam boṅga — Spirit of the dead village headman

Maraṅ Buru — God of the hill, A major supernatural spirit

Matkom — Madhuca latifolia Roxb

Mõrẽko — The five spirits of the sacred-grove, Santal men-folk, village officials

Mundari — Language of the Munda tribe

N

Naeke — Village priest

N'epel — Bride and groom seeing each other face-to-face

Nim dak' mandi — Margoza leaf boiled rice-water, birth purification ceremony

N'ir bolok' bap'la — Marriage by a girl forcefully getting into a boy's house as his wife

O

Ojha — Witch-doctor

Ojok' — To anoint

Or arder bap'la — Marriage by a boy forcefully taking a girl into his house to be his wife

Oṛak' — House

Oṛak' boṅga — House-Spirit

Oṛak' duaṛ n'el	Official visitation of girl's party to the house of the boy before the wedding is fixed

P

Pạn'jhi	The upper garment of Santal women (a traditional dress of the Santals)
Parhat	Lungi worn by Santal men and women (a traditional dress of the Santals)
Pargana Bura	The Spirit of the Pargana
Pargana	A division of the country, an over-chief of several adjacent Santal villages
Paranik	Administrative assistant to the village head-man
Peṛa-hor	Guest
Pilchu-haṛam	The first man, Adam
Pilachu-buṛhi	The first woman, Eve
Porob	Feast, festival

R

Raebarić	Match-maker
Rạskạ	Joy, Happiness
Rengeć din	Days of hunger

S

Saib sasawals	Collection of revenue in Santal Parganas

Saṅgha bap'la	Marriage between a widow and a widower
Santali	Language of the Santals
Sapha	Clean
Sapha-hoṛ	Clean man, Those who do not eat meat
Sarjom	Sal tree, Sacred tree of the Santals
Sarjom baha	Flower of Sarjom tree
Sasaṅ	Yellow, Turmeric
Savara	Language of a hill tribe in Santal Parganas
Sendra	Hunt, search
Simạ	Boundary
Simạ boṅga	Spirit of the boundary
Sing Boṅga	God Supreme
Sindur	Vermilion
Sindradhan	Marriage sealing ceremony
Sohrae	Month of Sohrae, Harvest festival

T

Taben jom	Eatting pressed rice, Official visit of the girl's party of the boy's house
Ṭaka cal	Ceremony in which the payment of the bride-price takes place

Thakurjiu	The God Supreme of the Santals (the name popULARy used by the Santals)
Ṭunki dipil bap'la	Marriage at groom's place by the bride carrying gifts in a basket to the groom's house.

Select Bibliography

Alixala, Jerome (ed.), Justice with Faith Today, Gujarat Sahitya, Prakash, Anand, 1981.

Amaladoss, M (ed.), Theologizing in India, TPI, Bangalore, 1981.

Arokiasamy, S (ed.), Liberation in Asia, Gujarat Sahitya Prakash, Anand, 1987.

Avila, Rafael, Worship and Politics, Orbis, New York, 1981

Biswas, P.C., Santals of the Santal Parganas, Bharatiya Adimjati Sevak Sangh, Delhi, 1956.

Boff, Leonardo, Jesus Christ Liberator, SPCK, England, 1987.

———, The Lord's Prayer, Orbis, New York, 1979.

Bompas, C. Henry (tr.) Folk-lore of the Santal Parganas, Ajoy Book Service, New Delhi, 1981.

Butter W. Robert, The Theology of Creation, The Mercier Press, Cork, 1969.

Cassidy, J. Richard, Jesus, Politics and Society, Orbis, New York, 1980.

Chaudhuri, A. B., The Santals—Religion and Rituals, Ashish Publ. House, New Dhlhi, 1987.

———, Witch Killings Amongst Santals, Ashish Publ. House, New Delhi, 1984.

Chaudhuri, Indu Roy, Folk Tales of the Santals, Sterling Publ. Ltd., Bangalore, 1982.

Cone, James H., A Black Theology of Liberation, Orbis, New York, 1986.

Culshaw, W.J., Tribal Heritage, Lutterworth Press, London, 1949.

Chotrae D.R. Katha (ed.). The Literature Committee of the Nor not-thern Evangelical Lutheran Church, The Mission Press, Benagaria, 1986.

Datta, Kalikinkar, The Santal Insurrection of 1855-57, University of Calcutta, Calcutta, 1940.

Driver, Tom F., Christ in a Changing World, SCM, Press, London, 1981.

Ellacuria, Ignacio, Freedom Made Flesh, Orbis, New York, 1976.

Fichtner, Joseph, Man the Image of God, Alba House, New York, 1978.

Gottwald, K. Norman (ed.) The Bible and Liberation, Orbis, New York, 1984.

Gutierrez, Gustavo, A Theology of Liberation, SCM Press, London, 1983.

Heschel, J. Abraham, The Prophets, Harper & Row, New York, 1962.

Horkoren, M.H.R. Katha (ed.), The Santal Mission of the Northern Churches, The Mission Press, Benagaria, 1928.

Hunter, A.M., The Works and Words of Jesus, SCM Press, London, 1971.

Koomar, C.H., Itihas, The Mission Press, Benagaria, 1987.

McCann, P. Dennis, Christian Realism and Liberation Theology, Orbis, New York, 1982.

Mukherjee, Charulal, The Santals, A. Mukherjee & Co. Pvt. Ltd., Calcutta, 1962.

Murmu H. Stephen, Hor Bap'la Puthi (Pahil hatin'), The Mission Press, Benagaria, 1961.

Niekle, F. Keith, The Synophtic Gospels, SCM Press, London, 1982.

O'Grady, F. John, Christian Anthropology, Paulist Press, Mahwah, N.J., 1976.

O'Malley, L.S.S., Bihar District Gazetters—Santal Parganas, Logos Press, New Dehli, 1984.

Orans, Martin, The Santal, A Tribe in Search of a Great Tradition, Wayne State Univ. Press, Detroit, 1965.

Puthanangady, Paul, Towards an Indian Theology of Liberation, ITA, Bangalore, 1986.

Rapaj, R.R.K , Harmawak' Ato, The Printing House, Calcutta, 1946.

Ray, P.O., Socio Cultural Process and Psychological Adatpation of the Santal, (Anthropological Survey of India), Govt. of India, Calcutta, 1975.

Ray, Tarapada (comp.), Santal Rebellion Documents, Subarnarekha, Calcutta, 1983.

Segundo. Juan Luis, The Sacraments Today, Redwood Burn Ltd., London, 1973.

——— -, The Liberation of Theology, Orbis, New York, 1977.

Sen, Suchibrata, The Santals of Jungle Mahals, Ratna Prakashan, Calcutta, 1984.

Skrefsrud, L.O., The Traditions and Institutions of the Santals, The Mission Press, Benagaria, 1968.

Sobrino, John, Christology at the Cross-Roads, SCM Press, London, 1978.

Somers, E. George, The Dynamics of Santal Traditions in a Peasant Society, Abhinav Publ., New Delhi, 1977.

Troisi, J., The Santals, 10 vols, ISI, Delhi, 1979.

Khan, Mumtaz Ali	Social Legislation and the Rural Poor.	50.00
Krishnakumari, N.S.	Status of Single Women in India.	125.00
Manuelraj. V.	A Santal Theology of Liberation.	150.00
Mandal, B.B.	Tribals at the Polls.	90.00
Madan, J.C.	Indian Police.	110.0
Mandavdhare, S.M.	Caste and land Relations in India	310.00
Menon, M. Indu	Status of Muslim Women in India.	50.00
Misra. R.G. and Gurvinder Kaur	Reservation Policy and Personnel Selection,	275.00
Mishra, Upendra	Caste and Politics in India.	225.00
Nischal, Surendra	Effective Leadership : A Study of White Collar Workers' Union Leaders.	145.00
Mishra, S.N. and Kushal Sharma	Problems and Prospects of Rural Development in India.	80.00
Mohan N. Shantha	Status of Nurses in India.	60.00
Narayana, E.A.	Voluntary Organisations and Rural Development in India.	225.00
Mohan, S. Shantha	Status of Banjara Women in India.	125.00
Omprakash, S.	Development of the Weaker Sections : Problems, Policies and Issues.	150.00
Paliwal, M.R.	Social Change and Education	175.00
Pai Panandiker, V.A. and Ajay K. Mehra	People's Participation in Family Planning.	160.00
Pai Panandiker, V.A. R.N. Bishnoi and O.P. Sharma	Organisational Policy for Family Planning.	125.00

Pai Panandiker, V.A. and P.N. Chaudhuri	Demographic Transition in Goa and its Policy Implications.	40.00
Pandey, K.K.	Rural Development in India : Continuity and Change.	125.00
Pillai, G. Narayana	Social Background of Political Leadership in India.	90.00
Rajgopal, P.R.	Communal Violence in India.	140.00
———	Social Change and Violence : the Indian Experience.	210.00
———	Violence and Response : A Critique of the Indian Criminal Justice System.	250.00
Rastogi, P.N.	India 1981-86 : A forecaste on Economic, Political and Social Developments.	50.00
Ray, B. Datta	The Emergence and Role of Middle Class in North-East India.	100.00
———	The Pattern and Problems of Population in North-East India.	250.00
Rita, Khanna	Agricultural Mechanisation and Social Change in India.	125.00
Rozario, M. Rita.	Trafficking in Women and Children in India.	125.00
Sachchidananda and Sihua, R P.	Education and the Disadvantaged : A Study of Scheduled Castes and Tribes.	275.00
Saksena, H.S.	Safeguards for Scheduled Caste and Tribes : Founding Father's View.	200.00
Samanta, R.K.	Rural Development in North-East India : Perspectives. Issues and Experiences	350.00

Seshadri, K.	Studies in Indian Polity.	150.00
———	Studies in the Problems of the Third World.	175.00
Sharma, Bharti	Juvenile Delinquents and their Social Culture.	175.00
Sharma, P.D.	Police, Internal Security and Developmental Disorder in India.	250.00
———	Police and Criminal Jutice Administration in India.	125.00
———	Police, Polity and People in India.	125.00
Sharma, R.N. and Santosh Bakshi	Tribes and Tribal Development : Select Bibliography.	250.00
Sinha, R.P.	Social Dimensions of Trade Unionism in India.	90.00
Singh, D.R.	Social Inequality in Leadership.	145.00
Singh, K.P.	Tribal Development in India.	325.00
Singh, S.N.	Reservation : Problem and Prospects	25.00
Singh, S.S.	Administration of Natural Justice in India.	250.00
Singh, S.S. and S. Sundram	Emerging Harijan Elite : A Study of their Identity.	125.00
Stobart, J.W.H	Islam and its Founder.	225.00
Trivedi. B.V.	Prison Administation in India.	120.00
Varma, B *IPS*	Insurgency and Counter-Insurgency.	225.00
Wishwakarma, R.K.	Urban and Regional Planning Policy in India.	75.00